and other kernels of truth

E. Lonnie Melashenko
and David B. Smith

Pacific Press Publishing Association
Boise, Idaho
Oshawa, Ontario, Canada

Edited by Jerry D. Thomas
Designed by Dennis Ferree
Cover photo by © Sinclair Studios

Library of Congress Cataloging-in-Publication Data

Melashenko, E. Lonnie.
Popcorn, the pearly gates, and other kernels of truth / E. Lonnie Melashenko and David B. Smith.
p. cm.
ISBN 0-8163-1347-4 (pbk. : alk. paper)
1. Justification—Popular works. 2. Good works (Theology)—Popular works. 3. Seventh-day Adventists—Doctrines—Popular works. I. Smith, David B., 1955 . II. Title.
BT764.2.M46 1996
248.4—dc20 96-13827
CIP

96 97 98 99 00 • 5 4 3 2 1

Contents

SECTION 1

A Debate With the Apostle James

CHAPTER 1

A Popcorn Ticket to Heaven

A new kind of Christian theology has recently been introduced to America by one of our leading popcorn manufacturers. Have you seen the TV commercial where a nervous saint standing at the gate to heaven is almost denied entrance?

"You've been eating the wrong kind of popcorn," the white-haired, white-robed, silver-haloed guard accuses, "laden with fat and cholesterol!"

"No!" the woman protests. "It wasn't the bad-fat kind. It was Orville Redenbacher's new, fat-free, low-calorie, low-cholesterol, healthy kind of popcorn now available in supermarkets everywhere."

Well, the guard and his sidekick push a button and roll the videotape. Sure enough, the brand name clearly shows that our faithful friend was indeed eating the good kind of popcorn. "We're so sorry," apologizes the heavenly guard.

"Please proceed." By the narrowest of margins, the fortunate popcorn eater avoids being sent down below to the nether regions where the deep-fat fry machines are operating. Instead, *because she's been good*, she gets to enter heaven.

Now, here at the *Voice of Prophecy*, we're really not that concerned about dissecting the Redenbacher Gospel. But this TV commercial's spiritual teachings actually parallel the beliefs that many faithful Christians have today. "Do the right thing, eat the right popcorn, do the best you can—that's the ticket to a heavenly mansion. It's what you do that counts."

A recent book in my denomination came out with the title, *Who's Got the Truth?* Five leading theologians from my faith tradition, all of them excellent Bible scholars, all of them with substantial "followings," thousands of people who read their books and see eye to eye with their teachings . . . had their slant on the gospel message dissected and analyzed.

And it all came down to this question: What Does It Take to Be Saved? Do you need to eat the right popcorn? Or do you simply say at one time in your life, "Jesus Christ, Son of God, I accept You as my Saviour"? Can you make one "faith statement" and be assured of eternal life?

Or is there a middle road? Or four or five middle roads?

In the book of James, probably as much as in any book of the Word of God, this theory battle rages. James is the springboard for many, many discussions and debates. What is this biblical writer really saying about what it takes to be saved?

There are actually three verses in this controversial book that "rattle people's cages" more than just about anything. In James, chapter 2, verse 14, the writer says this: "What good is it, my brothers, if a man claims to have faith but has no deeds? Can such faith save him?"

In the two verses following this universal question, James

really gets down to the old brass tacks. Listen as he amplifies: "Suppose a brother or sister is without clothes and daily food. If one of you says to him, 'Go, I wish you well; keep warm and well fed,' but does nothing about his physical needs, what good is it?"

He then concludes with the second of our killer statements. Here it is in 2:17: "In the same way, faith by itself, *if it is not accompanied by action*, is dead."

You may recognize this warning better in the familiar King James: "Faith without works is dead."

If you're not spiritually reeling already, let me add the third of James's plain statements. "You see that a person is justified by what he *does* and not by faith alone" (2:24).

How does this square with the hallmark *Voice of Prophecy* text we're always quoting from Ephesians 2? The one which states that sinful mankind is saved by the grace of God and *not* by his good works? You remember: "For it is by grace you have been saved, through faith—and this not of yourselves, it is the gift of God—not by works, so that no one can boast" (2:8).

It would appear at first glance that these two Bible writers simply don't agree and never could agree. Throw them into a WWF (World Wrestling Federation) ring and let them thrash it out . . . because they can't both be right. Maybe we have to be either "Paul Christians" or "James Christians."

Is it any wonder that many Christian ministers have simply stopped preaching from the book of James? Their congregations can't handle it, and they can't handle it either.

I read a Christian bestseller that goes back a few years, and the author, a leading evangelical pastor, said that with his prayer meeting group, they had to lay this difficult book of James to one side. They weren't ready to address it. He had tried once and, as he put it, people were bleeding all over the aisles—figuratively speaking, of course. Their assurance of salvation was flying right out of the stained-glass window.

Well, I'm not going to pretend that in a few short chapters here, we can solve a two-thousand-year-old Christian debate. That would be foolish of me, and foolish of you if you bought into my arrogance. This is a discussion that's gone on for a long time and will continue long after you set down this volume. But I don't believe we should be afraid to explore the book of James. That would be equally foolish. I always trust in the God who inspired the book of James, because He's the same God who supervised the process that brought this book into the holy canon of Scriptures. This is a book we're meant to read and explore and debate and live.

Let me make another point as we embark on our journey. James is meant to be a book of encouragement among friends, a provider of positive exhortation. Fifteen times in these five short chapters, James refers to his readers as "brothers," which includes you and me today. It's meant to bring us along, as well-beloved family members, closer and closer to God's ideal for our lives. Would you accept that?

With that in mind, let's explore some of the givens that all of us can subscribe to at the outset. It's very clear from all of Scripture that obedience and good works are important. God calls us to obey; that's a consistent theme going right from Genesis through the Old Testament, into the New Testament, through the Gospels, through the Epistles, and into the book of Revelation.

Let's look together at Revelation 12 where God's saints of the very last days are described. And who does the Bible say they are? "Those who obey God's commandments and hold to the testimony of Jesus" (vs. 17).

In 1 John 2:4 we read this in the familiar King James: "He that saith, I know him [Christ], and keepeth not his commandments, is a liar, and the truth is not in him."

In fact, we find in the teachings of Jesus Himself that good works are important, even necessary. In the well-known

"Sheep and Goats" parable that you can read in Matthew 25, it describes a scene where all people on earth are divided up into two groups in the end. And then they're judged . . . based on *what*?

Just go down the list as detailed in verses 35 and 36. There are those who fed the hungry, gave water to a thirsty stranger, provided hospitality, clothed the naked, and visited the prisoner. And these people on the right hand, the sheep, are judged to be worthy of heaven because of that list of good deeds.

Now, that passage doesn't explicitly state that the fulfilling of this checklist was then the *basis* of their salvation, that they had earned salvation by their deeds. Those two verses don't erase Calvary out of the Bible. But apparently the cups of cold water and kindness to strangers are part of the evidence that's considered.

How, then, should we feel about these cups of water? What is their role, their function, in the plan of salvation? Could you be saved without them? What is a Christian who says he has faith, but then never bothers to even try to obey? Is he still a Christian? Not a Christian anymore? A bad Christian? Or was he ever a Christian?

As we keep our Bibles open during this study, we'll try to allow God's Word to answer these very hard questions. The answers we'll look for together are what divide huge, global denominations from each other—so this is no trivial matter.

But let me say this: Here at the *Voice of Prophecy*, we never want to stray from Calvary. We never want to move away from the foot of the cross of Jesus. That cross is *the* basis, the only basis, of our salvation today. That's not only a Bible truth, it's an unchangeable, unshakeable, non-negotiable truth. We put on our hiking boots and pick up our lanterns, and we start from there.

Are you ready? May God help us as we explore what He would have us to understand.

CHAPTER 2

One More Vote for Nurse Ratchet

In the 1975 Oscar-winning film based on the book, *One Flew Over the Cuckoo's Nest*, there's a scene where antihero R. P. McMurphy is determined that he and the other patients in the mental hospital want to switch the daily schedule so they can watch the World Series on the ward's tiny black-and-white TV set. The supervisor in charge—remember the famous Nurse Ratchet?—agrees to put the matter to a vote. But out of nine men in the therapy group, McMurphy only gets two or three votes.

The next day, though, he's back again. After an evening of tough political campaigning, he's sure he has the troops all lined up. Again, Nurse Ratchet agrees to a vote on whether to watch Game Two. This time all nine hands go up.

Then this tough head nurse really pulls a mean one on Randle. "I'm sorry," she tells him. "I only count nine votes."

"That's right," he crows in triumph. "It's a landslide."

Amazingly, she then informs him that she's counting every man on the ward, not just those in the therapy group. All eighteen men count, even those who are standing over in a corner staring idly into space or mumbling to themselves.

"You're counting *them*?"

"That's right," she tells him. "All those men count too."

"OK, just hang on, then," McMurphy says. "All I need is one more vote." And for the next few minutes, actor Jack Nicholson goes from man to man, imploring them to vote. "Just raise your hand," he begs them, one after the other. "Don't you want to watch the World Series, fella? Just stick up that hand." He knows that the men don't understand, that they don't comprehend what they might be voting on, or that they would mean what they're voting. He just wants one more hand raised in the air. It's a sad and desperate little scene.

And maybe, just maybe, it's that kind of empty, nonmeaningful voting that the Bible writer James is referring to when he pens an expression like: "Faith without works is dead."

You and I are earnestly trying to discover what this very difficult book is really talking about. Over and over, James *seems* to be telling us how important obedience is, how vital and necessary good deeds and Christian actions are. We almost come to the point where we begin to say, "Maybe simple faith in Jesus Christ isn't enough. Maybe what I do counts as well."

And when we come over to James 2:24, we almost do sink the ship. Let's look at it again: "You see that a person is justified by what he does and not by faith alone."

How does this square with the much-proclaimed Protestant Christian message which basically reads like this: "Justification through grace alone, by faith alone, in Christ alone, nothing else being necessary"?

Let me repeat those last four words: "Nothing Else Being Necessary." But what about obedience? And the works a man or woman *does*? James says they *are* necessary. So where do we go from here? Are we already lost? We've started out on a journey of discovery, and have our lanterns burned out already?

Deep down in our hearts, we know that to simply raise our hands and blankly say, "OK, I accept Jesus"—and then not do anything about it . . . well, we know that approach misses the mark. There's more to the Christian life than just saying one sentence one time.

Have you ever witnessed a beach baptism? They're not so common now, but back in the 1970s, I can well recall how people right down here on the shores of the Pacific Ocean would hear a blue-jeaned man standing there in the sand give them a sermon. And then they'd be baptized. Fifty or a hundred of them at a time would wade into the water and be baptized. In fact, sometimes onlookers who'd just come onto the scene at the last moment, and maybe didn't even hear the sermon, would go out there into the water and be baptized too.

But what happens after you come up out of the water? What happens the next day? And the next week? Is one trip to the beach enough—"nothing else being necessary"? Or, as James seems to say, is faith dead if it doesn't lead to good works? Is an expression of faith meaningless, like that empty, uncomprehending vote for R. P. McMurphy's World Series, if we don't follow it up with a sufficient pile of good deeds?

Let me take you deeper into some very hard thinking. Have you ever seen a very public Christian, a well-known believer, or media evangelist who openly expressed their faith in God? And then it came out that they had been cheating on their wife? Or that they'd been involved in blackmail and coverups and hush money? We've all heard these stories, haven't we? And what did we automatically think? You probably said to yourself something like, "Huh! Faith without works is dead." Didn't you? Deep in our hearts we know that the words we *say* aren't enough in themselves.

Not long ago, when the Susan Smith trial in South Carolina finished up, we heard about an older relative who had been sexually involved with her for years. This man had abused her when she was younger, and right up to shortly before her crime of murder had continued in a consensual relationship with this tragically confused young woman. And as you remember, this man was a prominent Christian in the community, a member of one of the more well-known religious/political coalition groups here in the United States. And we all said to ourselves, along with James: "What good is faith without deeds? Something is the matter here!"

Let me share with you my very personal convictions. You know, there are real words, and there are empty words. There's real voting, and there's blind voting. And, frankly, there's a real kind of faith, and there's empty, meaningless faith. And it's empty, *false* faith that doesn't lead to anything.

Dr. John Ankerberg, Christian apologist, has this to say: "Works do not bring justification, but they do flow from it. Works are the results that show that a man has a true and genuine faith. So a faith that has no works is a dead faith. It is not genuine."

What do you think of that? Do you agree? As James says in chapter 2, what does it mean if you pat a starving child on the head and say, "Well, I'm sorry, kid. Good luck to you. Hang in there. I'll pray for you" . . . and you don't do anything to feed him or her? Those words don't mean a thing if you don't follow them up with some loving action.

Here's another observation from Ankerberg: "This is why Luther said, 'Justification is by faith alone, but not by the faith that *is* alone.' By this he meant, first, justification is secured solely on the basis of Christ and what He did at the cross, not by our works. Second, genuine faith will always result in good works flowing from it."

Ephesians 2:10, which follows our favorite grace verses in 8 and 9, makes this plain. Because of the gift of grace: "We are God's workmanship, created in Christ Jesus to do good works."

It's interesting and sobering that the Bible tells us how faith is more than words. It's more than a baptism trip to the Pacific Ocean; it's more than nodding your head and agreeing that something is true. I like how The Living Bible, which is a paraphrase rendition, puts James 2:19: "Are there still some among you who hold that 'only believing' is enough? Believing in one God? Well, remember that the demons believe this too—so strongly that they tremble in terror!"

Yes, it's plain that Christianity is more than believing and thinking—it's also doing. All through the four Gospels, Jesus, time and time again, talks about what a Christian believer will *do*. Turn back to the Sermon on the Mount, Matthew 5–7, and you find many, many verses on Christian living, on unselfishness and controlling your anger, on being faithful to your spouse, and on going the second mile. And then in chapter 7, Jesus says this: "By their *fruit* you will recognize them."

Which reminds us of what we read in the previous chapter of this book about the righteous Judge, who divides people into two groups and then makes His determination as He sees who among them was kind to strangers and visited the sick and gave food to the hungry and water to the thirsty.

Yes, real faith will lead to obedience and good works. Real faith is accompanied by real growth; real faith brings forth real fruit.

But now we turn again to the heart of this debate. As we talk about the good works praised so highly by James and

Jesus, . . . are these in any way the *basis* of our salvation? Are we saved *because* of our obedience? Can we lose salvation if we don't bother to obey?

And here's another hard question. If a Christian has faith, or says he has faith, but doesn't exhibit these good works, did he ever really have that faith? Was he lying? Or deceived?

This is where the battle lines are really drawn! We're getting right to the point in the path where we hear the clanking of the spears and the rattling of swords. Chapter 3 should be very interesting! Don't go wandering off.

CHAPTER 3

Herman's Matrimonial Obligations

The day Herman got married, his older brother, who was wise in the ways of married love, took him aside before the ceremony. "Little brother," he said, "if you really love your wife, you'll kiss her every day. Never forget that: every day, you kiss her. That's what people who love each other do."

Well, that sounded fine. Herman already had in mind that he was planning to kiss his wife every day anyway. He agreed with his brother that such a thing would spring up naturally in the heart of a man who really loved his bride.

But during the wedding ceremony, as the preacher went on and on for about an hour and fifteen minutes, it came across a bit differently. "Herman, you've *got* to kiss your wife every day," the preacher exhorted him. "That's what's expected of married men; that's what it's all about. You've got to do it; this is the requirement of holy matrimony. So be sure you fulfill this obligation. In fact, if you don't, I'll track you down next week and rip up your marriage certificate."

Whoa! That was kind of a heavy thought. And it got even more challenging when the bride's mother took him off to one side during the wedding reception and began to lecture him about the importance of kissing his new wife every day. "Let me tell you something, son," she said. "If you want to *stay* in relationship with my daughter, then kissing her every day is the way to do that. Not that it's a hard-and-fast requirement like the preacher said, but plenty of kissing and romance will hold the two of you in your love relationship." She took a bite of wedding cake before continuing. "So be sure you do it!"

Well, Herman went on his honeymoon feeling just a little bit discouraged and confused. Everyone had told him the same thing: "Herman, kiss your wife." And the irony of it all was this: He'd always intended to kiss his wife every day! He loved her! But now, with all of these conflicting theories ringing in his ears, he wasn't sure anymore if he was kissing her for the right reasons.

I apologize for taking the gospel message and trying to illustrate it with a very trivial story. But do you know—this is really where many Christians find themselves as they study this important issue of faith and works. So many theologies all say the same thing: "It's good to obey." All right . . . in fact, we were planning to obey anyway. After all, we love God and want to please Him. We want to follow Jesus, our Example. But now, along with Herman, we have to start asking ourselves: Why? What is the role of obedience in the Christian faith?

Right now we want to key on two Bible verses, written by two different Bible warriors. The first is Romans 3:28, which was written, of course, by Paul. "We maintain that a man is justified by faith *apart* from observing the Law."

OK. Now let's cross over to the other side of the war theater and read from James 2:24. Here's his statement: "You see that a man is justified by works, and *not* by faith alone."

So there you have it. "Justified by faith apart from works." Or . . . "Justified by works, and not by faith alone." A mathematician would say that these are mutually exclusive statements. At most, only one of them could be true.

And we face the same irony here that our blushing bridegroom, Herman, is looking at. Both Paul and James believe in good works. In fact, when you start reading in Paul's book of Romans, you barely get to the fifth verse when he already says this: "Through him [Jesus Christ] and for his name's sake, we received grace and apostleship to call people from among all the Gentiles to the *obedience* that comes from faith."

Over in chapter 3 of the same book: "Do we, then, nullify the law by this faith? Not at all! Rather, we uphold the law" (verse 31). Chapter 6: "Shall we go on sinning so that grace may increase? By no means" (verse 1).

It sounds as though both of them are saying, "Obedience is great. And vital. And necessary. You better do it." But only one of them, James, seems to go on to say that obedience is partly the *basis* for being justified, or being saved.

In Herman's case, both the older brother and the preacher are saying, "Kiss your wife, man!" But only the minister is claiming that the performing of this deed is what he's going to *base* the continuing marriage relationship on.

Well, our friend Herman—and all of us looking on—might well ask: "What's the difference? Either way, you've got to kiss your wife." And in our case: "What's the difference? Either way, you've got to obey. If the end conclusion is the same, isn't all the rest a lot of hot-air theology?"

I don't believe so. And when we get right down to it, I believe we can find beautiful evidence that Paul and James are essentially in agreement.

In a very important book entitled *Protestants & Catholics:*

Do They Now Agree? John Ankerberg and John Weldon very carefully explore the word *justify* in the two "warring" texts I mentioned earlier. "A man is justified by faith alone." "A man is justified by his works, and *not* by faith alone." Do Paul and James mean the same thing with those words? And, of course, the title of Ankerberg's book indicates what a huge and global debate this can be, with entire faith systems basing their theology on how this discussion comes out.

In the book of Romans, when Paul uses the word *justify*, coming from the Greek *dikaio*, the meaning is that of being fully acquitted or brought into right standing. Your secular dictionary would say, "Declared free of blame, absolved." In fact, our American Heritage Dictionary includes an openly theological definition for the word *justify*, and says this: "To free (a human being) of the guilt and penalty attached to grievous sin." And then adds: "Used only of God."

Of course, this concept of being acquitted or declared righteous or "brought into right standing" *is* the heart of our salvation. That is it! What Jesus Christ did for us at Calvary brings us into right standing with God, and Paul is absolutely correct in stating that we're justified *by faith alone*.

Now before we go over to the book of James, take a little detour with me to Luke 7:35. After describing the inconsistencies of those who criticized both Jesus and John the Baptist, Jesus says this: "But wisdom is justified of all her children" (KJV). Same word, same original Greek word, same everything.

But we discover an entirely different meaning. Jesus isn't saying here that wisdom is being brought into right standing by her children. No, instead He is simply saying that wisdom is proved right or vindicated by the fruit it produces. In fact, listen to the same verse as rendered in the NIV: "But wisdom is *proved right* by all her children."

In the Good News Bible: "God's wisdom is *shown to be true* by all who accept it."

In the NASB: "God's wisdom is *vindicated*."

So back to our troublesome text in James. Here it is again: "You see that a man is *justified* by what he does and not by faith alone."

And you know, as you read this entire chapter 2, where James is talking about empty faith, meaningless faith, where a religious person pats a starving person on the head and says, "Poor fellow. Blessings on you" . . . but won't lift a finger to help him, he now comes to our verse and says very clearly: "Your works show or vindicate what kind of faith you have. Your acts of true kindness prove that you have real faith, not empty faith."

James used *justify* to describe how faith and works are related before a watching world. Paul uses *justify* to describe our standing before a holy God. The justification James spoke of isn't the basis of our salvation. But our obedience does "justify" or show or demonstrate to the watching world that we have a faith experience with God that is real. Real faith shows itself in good works.

And do you know something? When we pop out a definition of the word *justify* with our new CD-ROM encyclopedia, this very definition shows up: "To demonstrate or prove to be just, right, or valid."

So let me suggest to you that there is no war here! Both Paul and James are clear in saying several things: First, it is God's grace received through faith that saves us. Period. Second, obedience and good works are important. They're vital. They spring naturally from a faith experience. Although they do *not* save us, they are the natural fruit that occurs in a Christian life. And third, our obedience vindicates or proves that our faith is genuine and real.

We still have to ask ourselves: does it make a difference? We're still going to obey. We're still going to "kiss our wives." Does it matter what the motivation is? Basis-of-salvation or no-basis-of-salvation, does it matter? Our journey continues.

CHAPTER 4

"Pick a Church—Any Church"

Now I'd like to invite you to join a church. In fact, I'm going to give you several churches to choose from. Each of these, by the way, represents millions of believers, so I'm not asking you to join a tiny, out-of-the-way body of believers.

The first church you ought to consider is described by just four words: ***Saved By Faith Alone***.

In chapter two, we quoted what many consider to be the pure Protestant creed. Here it is again: *"Justification through grace alone, by faith alone, in Christ alone, nothing else being necessary."*

Now, do let me make one point. If you join this *Saved By Faith Alone* church, you need to understand that we're talking about real faith, genuine faith . . . the kind that does lead to obedience. So the words "nothing else being necessary" don't imply that following God's will isn't going to be important. If you join this "faith alone" church, you *will* be obeying. I just wanted you to know that.

Church number 2 has a slightly different wording on their sign out front. It reads this way: ***Saved By Faith, Exhibited Through Works***. These parishioners like how both Paul and James describe that our genuine faith—which is what saves us—will demonstrate itself or validate itself through obedience and goodness. So that's the name of this second church.

You may already want to protest and say, "But Lonnie, the way you've defined faith, this church and church number 1 are really one and the same." And you might have a good point . . . but let's continue looking through the Yellow Pages.

Church number 3 prints this on their bulletins: ***Saved By Faith, Kept in Relationship By Works***. In their view, a Christian's relationship in Christ is protected and nurtured and strengthened by his or her obedience, by walking with Christ. They look through the Bible and they see how disobedient believers often departed from their relationship with God because of their willful, flagrant sins. And so they like this description: *Saved By Faith, Kept in Relationship By Works* or obedience.

And yes, I can see you raising your hand again. "Uh, Lonnie, in my *Saved By Faith Alone* church, that kind of true obedience naturally helps keep me in a relationship with Jesus. What is there new here?" And again I would agree that you have scored a very good point. Maybe these three churches are actually one big "superchurch."

Would you like to visit church number 4? Here's its name: ***Saved By Faith Plus Works***.

I can already hear the rumble of the crowd. "Oh, dear," you say. "I don't like the sound of that so much." And in a way, this church's title does sound as if we're making the "works" half part of the *basis* of our salvation. And we've discovered how, in the Bible, both Paul and James were adamantly opposed to that way of thinking.

At the same time, it could well be argued that our obedience, as the *fruit* of salvation and as a vital part of what keeps us in a thriving relationship with God . . . well, maybe good works should be considered an integral part of the salvation process. But your objections are duly noted.

Here's the fifth church that's vying for your vote. ***Saved By Faith, Kept By Works***. "We're saved by faith alone," these members say. "But our obedience is necessary if we're going to maintain that salvation. If we accept Christ as our Saviour, and then willfully disobey Him, we wouldn't be safe to save in His kingdom." And maybe you might want to go back across the street to church number 3, ***Saved By Faith, Kept In Relationship By Works***, and see if really these are the same two churches. But let's visit our final church together.

Church number 6: ***Works Alone***. Just as there was a "faith alone" denomination, here on the other end of the spectrum, perhaps there is a "works alone" group as well. Faith in Christ's atoning blood isn't a part of the equation at all; their good lives and obedience to the Commandments are the *whole* story.

Well, friend, there you have it. Six options. And perhaps you can think of others. In fact, perhaps you see yourself as a two *and* a half, or maybe you might say, "Actually, Lonnie, I'm a one *and* a three." And I'll be the first to concede that there *is* a good deal of fuzzy crossover from one group to the next. How we define words and to what limit we take these definitions—is all part of what we perceive to be God's will for our lives.

Let me right away encourage you against one temptation. I hope you'll try to *not* identify these six descriptions with actual denominations. To hear, for example: ***Saved By Faith, Kept in Relationship By Works***—and immediately think, "Oh, that's the such-and-such church." I believe that in virtually every church, we struggle to grasp the pure gospel message and to understand in our own lives what it means to obey Jesus Christ. There are real Christians and lax Christians and works-oriented 100 percent legalists in every faith group.

Would you let me very humbly share some ideas that ought to be bedrock truths for each one of us? And please know how much I hope you join me in a humble spirit of learning. None of us is smart enough to fully understand everything in God's Word. But continued study is so important.

Here's principle number 1: Hang onto "faith in Jesus Christ" as your *sole basis* of salvation. Whatever role obedience plays in our lives, it is not the basis of salvation. We don't *earn* salvation by our works. Paul is clear on that. I believe James is clear on that. We cannot be saved on the basis of what we do; that is a foundational Christian truth. Take that away and the *Voice of Prophecy* would be off the air and totally shut down by tomorrow morning.

In Pope John Paul II's recent book, *Crossing the Threshold of Hope*, he makes this statement: "A good life is the *condition* of salvation."

Now, exactly what does he mean? I haven't read the entire book, and I wouldn't profess to know precisely. I will say that, as a Protestant Christian, I would not want to state the terms of salvation in that way.

Here's principle number 2: Obedience is important and vital. Jesus said so. Paul said so. James for sure said so. While works and commandment keeping are not the root of our salvation, they are most assuredly the *fruit* of our faith relationship. Obedience comes naturally and spontaneously and willingly from a person who has faith in God. Sometimes through great hardship and embattled resolve, as we see in the Garden of Gethsemane. But still from a motivation of love and loyalty.

Here's a third principle: Whether you put it in your church's nameplate or not, obedience *will* be exhibited in the life. Maybe you've read in the book of John where Jesus says—and this is King James: "If ye love me, keep my commandments" (14:15).

But you know, I much prefer the New International Version's way of putting that verse. It actually comes across as a promise rather than as a command. Notice: "If you love me, you *will obey* what I command."

You can almost hear Jesus adding these words: "And you'll love doing it!"

Allow me to add, if you will, to principle number 3. I'll say this as well: If you are indeed saved by faith, your obedience *will*, without a doubt, help to keep you in relationship with Jesus. Obedience is a beautiful protection of a friendship; good deeds nurture and safeguard a love relationship. Whether you put it in the title or not, if your faith in Christ is a real faith, your obeying will have that effect.

And one further observation. I wouldn't want to pick a church title which gave any implication that we *didn't* need to obey. On the one hand, we don't want to say that obedience is the basis of salvation. But equally dangerous would be to say, "Hey, no need to even try."

And you know, there are those who make that very suggestion. "Faith in Christ is all-important," they say. But in their very next sentence they add: "But keeping the Commandments is not possible *or* necessary." At that point we would have to say along with James: "What kind of faith is that?"

But here are some thought questions designed to get you to turn the page! First, if we join one or the other of these churches I've mentioned here, can we be assured of salvation? What do obedience and the importance of good works imply with regard to our confidence?

Next question: If faith in Christ is *the* basis of our salvation, then why do we so often read in the Bible about God judging people based on their good works? The sheep and the goats . . . feeding the hungry and clothing the naked . . . "Here are they who keep the Commandments of God." What about that?

Our journey still has a way to go, doesn't it? We're glad you're along for the trip.

CHAPTER 5

A Girlfriend for Bob Hope

This chapter comes from a Friday program—and sometimes on Friday, we let down our hair a little bit on the *Voice of Prophecy*. So I know you're going to forgive me if we begin with an old bit of comedy shtick from a young fellow named Bob Hope.

In one of his old black-and-white "road" pictures with Bing Crosby, Hope has a heavy-duty romantic interest in a particular young woman. Unfortunately, her feelings for him aren't quite so generous. At one point in this one-way romance, he says to her father: "Your daughter's in love with me."

Well, she almost explodes in disgusted protest. "I love YOU?!!"

And Bob Hope smiles contentedly. "See? She admits it!"

You know, some people are happy to hear those three words, no matter what tone of voice they may come in. But most of us are looking for something deeper. We want "I love you" to really mean "I love you."

I guess it's possible for our lips to repeat words like "I love you," or, maybe, something like "I'm sorry" . . . and our body English says something entirely different. Or our actions may sing a completely different tune.

I think, in a way, that answers the question we posed at the end of chapter 4. If faith in God is the basis of our salvation, then why is biblical judgment so often described in terms of our deeds, our actions? We've already mentioned the famous "sheep and goats" parable where the heavenly Judge passes out sentences *based* on acts of kindness—cold water given away and prisoners visited, and so forth. In other words, a judgment based on works. In fact, there is no other kind of judgment explicitly taught in the Old or New Testaments.

Actually, there's more. Turn back to chapter 7 of Matthew, and in our NIV Study Bible, the subtitle for that section is called "Judging Others." In verse 2, Jesus promises: "In the same way you judge others, you will be judged."

Tell me. Do you and I ever judge others based on behavior and works? We do it all the time, don't we? Move down to verse 20 of that same chapter, where Christ is talking about a tree and its fruit. He makes this statement: "By their fruit you will recognize them."

Who's he talking about? Christians. People who claim to be "spiritual." The next paragraph has something to say to Bob Hope and to us about empty "I love you" words. Listen: "Not everyone who says to me, 'Lord, Lord,' will enter the kingdom of heaven, but only he who does the will of my Father who is in heaven. Many will say to me on that day, 'Lord, Lord, did we not prophesy in your name, and in your name drive out demons and perform many miracles?' Then I will tell them plainly, 'I never knew you. Away from me, you evildoers!' "

And you can turn to the very last page in your Bible, Revelation 22, and find a judgment *against* those who aren't saved. Who are they? Murderers and idolaters and adulterers and people who love falsehoods. In other words, people judged on the basis of what they did or didn't do.

Very likely you and I are made somewhat uncomfortable reading about a judgment based on our deeds. But let me ask you this. If true, genuine faith always goes with obedience, then is it legitimate for the Judge to look at the obedience as a means of seeing if the faith is genuine? In other words, if A *always* leads to B, then you could judge correctly based on either A *or* B.

But you protest: "God knows the heart! Why should He look at works when He can see through to the inside and know that I'm sincere?"

Is it possible that judgment is just as much for us—and for watching worlds—as it is for God? How absolutely right you are that God knows all! He knows your outside; He knows your inside . . . and He's always known. There are no surprises for God. He doesn't have to stop and think when He comes to your name: "Should I save her? Hmmmmm; I have to think about this; let's look at all the evidence." God knows your heart and your every thought and secret attitude. But it's equally true that the life you've lived gives ample evidence of whether or not you've stayed in a genuine faith relationship with Jesus Christ.

Now let me ask you a very important and sobering question. Does this Bible topic rob us of our joy and of our assurance of salvation? We've often quoted 1 John 5:13 on the *Voice of Prophecy*. "I write these things to you who believe in the name of the Son of God so that you may *know* that you have eternal life."

Wonderful news—but have we just wiped it out? Can we ever read that verse on the air again? Does our discovery of the importance of obedience and of the *role* of obedience in the judgment erase our confidence? Can we only be confident Christians the first half hour after conversion?

Let me open my heart right now. As you know, the *Voice of Prophecy* does not teach or believe in the popular concept of "once saved, always saved." As we look carefully at *all* the Bible testimony, we don't believe the evidence is there to support the idea that once you give your life to Jesus Christ and enter into a relationship with Him . . . that you can never leave. I've known people who absolutely were walking with the Lord. They loved Him; they were serving Him; they had faith in Him. Then later—and it broke my heart to see it or hear about it—these men and women turned away. It's not that they momentarily stumbled and fell; these people completely rejected their relationship with Christ. They no longer had faith in Him.

I mentioned earlier John Ankerberg's book, *Catholics & Protestants: Do They Now Agree?* Now, this well-written book does take the view that a Christian can never lose his or her salvation. In other words: "Once saved, always saved."

But in one of the text notes, this interesting point is conceded: "Although Luther agreed that the merits of Christ were the sole basis of a man's justification, and that it did not depend in any way on a man's deeds, Luther still thought that a man could lose his justification if he totally and finally turned away from Christ."

Frankly, I believe Martin Luther had that one just right. I believe King David corroborated this truth when he prayed in Psalm 51: "*Restore* to me the joy of Your salvation."

Friend, *real* faith, genuine faith—the kind that Paul and James both recommended to us—is a trust relationship with God and with His Son, Jesus Christ. Let me say that again: it's a trust relationship.

When you enter into that relationship, *You Are Saved*! You are guaranteed a place in God's kingdom; your future, your eternity with God, is secure.

At that point, you begin to obey. That's what Paul and James have been telling us all along. Faith and works go together. You begin to obey naturally and gladly, because real faith is simply like that. You *want* to obey. And your obedience, your good works, do two things: they express and validate your faith, and they help keep you in that faith. Your obedience protects your faith experience.

Do you obey perfectly? Do you instantly attain some kind of perfect loyalty? No, you don't. Of course not. But because you love the Lord, you *stay* in that faith relationship, that trust connection. And our loving God makes it His responsibility to lead you toward perfect obedience and perfect trust according to His own timetable.

As long as you stay in that faith relationship, *You Are Saved*. You have assurance. Nothing can tear you away. Even on judgment day, as you have remained in that faith relationship, you are perfectly secure.

That doesn't mean that you can't tear *yourself* away. I believe God's Word makes it clear that you, yourself, can choose to depart from a trust relationship with God. God never forces a person to come to Him or to stay with Him. But unless you willfully determine to do that, you can live your Christian life in full assurance and joyful anticipation of eternal life.

As far as assurance is concerned, I honestly believe we have two choices. We can believe as I've just described, that faith is a relationship we enter into. And we stay in it by choosing to stay in it. We could leave at any time, but we never have to. If we choose to, we can have absolute assurance now and forever. To me, that sounds pretty good.

On the other hand, if we accept the concept of "Once saved, always saved"—I agree, that certainly sounds like assurance. But what happens to someone who believes that way and then later takes a radical departure from the Lord? And it's clear to everyone looking on that this is a man or woman who has completely left their faith relationship. As Martin Luther said, this person has "totally and finally turned away from Christ."

What I've heard too often is this comment: "Well, that person never *really* had faith in the first place. Something was wrong with their initial experience. That wasn't real faith."

What's the result, then, of this teaching? In my view, instead of giving assurance, it robs *all* of us of our confidence. It puts doubt in every heart. From that perspective, every single Christian would have to walk around all day, every day, wondering: "Is my faith real? Is it genuine? Could it someday crash and burn? I think I have faith, but do I really? Am I fooling myself?"

Well, that's how it looks from here. You may have a different view, and we certainly want you to know how much we love you. Write to us here at the *Voice of Prophecy* and let's continue this discussion.

In the end, let's keep our eyes on Jesus. Theories are interesting, but Jesus saves. Isn't that right? Discussions are helpful and enlightening, but it's the cross of Calvary, the sacrifice of our Saviour, that is our only hope.

And it's our Bible friend James, tough-talking, faith-and-works-preaching James, who brings us to our final thought. James 5:11 says: "The Lord is full of compassion and mercy."

Where would we be without that good news?

SECTION 2

Driver's Ed. for Christians

CHAPTER 6

Aim High in Steering

Do you remember driver's ed. class? You were probably fifteen years old at the time. For one whole semester of high school, you watched crash movies and learned about centrifugal force and banked curves and one-way turns and the vehicle code and the four strokes of a car engine's cylinders. Some of it was probably kind of interesting—and some boring—but driver's ed. was the one class where nobody ever quit! In fact, many high-school teachers have observed that generally driver's ed. is about the only class where every kid makes sure they pass. You *had* to pass driver's ed. . . . because that was your ticket to a driver's license.

Probably the biggest slogan in driver's ed. class, and it certainly has application to our Christian journey, is this: DEFENSIVE DRIVING. Looking out for the other guy, it's called. And your teacher told you, "There are a million lousy drivers out there who aren't looking out for you, so you've got to look out for them *and* yourself. You've got to protect yourself."

The story is told of a young man who didn't ever take driver's ed. One day, he was giving a ride to an older friend, who was understandably nervous about the trip. Traveling at a fairly high rate of speed, they began to approach an intersection just as the light turned yellow, then red. But instead of stopping, our young friend punched down on the gas pedal and roared through the glowing red light, just barely missing several cars and pedestrians.

"What's the matter with you?" the passenger yelled. "We could have been killed!"

But the driver just shrugged. "That's how my brother taught me to drive."

No driver's ed., you see.

They came up to another red light, and the same thing happened again—ninety miles an hour right through the red light; "That's how my brother taught me."

And this happened about four times in a row: blatantly driving right through red lights. "That's how my brother taught me." Over and over.

Well, by now the passenger was a total wreck, clawing on his seat belt and praying just to get home safely. Finally up ahead was a green light. Whew! "Thank goodness," he muttered to himself. "At least this time I can relax."

To his amazement, the young man came up to the intersection—and this time slammed on the brakes and came to a screeching halt, almost putting his friend through the windshield. "Now what?" the confused passenger asked. "It's green. Why don't you go?"

"I can't take that chance," the driver said. "My brother might be coming from the other direction."

Well, I guess a story like that makes us glad that driver's ed. is a mandatory course! But as we consider five vital rules of driving safety, I want you to join me in looking at the *biblical* truths behind them.

Aim High in Steering

Do you remember this driver's ed. list?

1. Aim high in steering.
2. Get the big picture.
3. Keep your eyes moving.
4. Make sure others see you.
5. Leave yourself an out.

What does it mean to "Aim high in steering"? Do you remember the first time you drove on the freeway, with your dad perspiring freely there in the passenger seat? And for the first couple of hours, all you did was *steer*. Steering the car was an endless and exhausting series of tiny little turns. A little to the left. No, that's too much. Back to the right. Then left. Then a little more left. Then over-correcting back to the right. Meanwhile, everyone in the car is seasick.

Probably you were using the edge of the car and the side of the road—or the center divider—as your guide. And to keep those two lined up was hard!

But after a few hours or a few days, you finally learned to let your eyes travel far up the road, and you simply steered toward that spot. Your hands learned to make automatic adjustments as you aimed *high* in steering.

On crowded freeways like we have here in southern California, you've *got* to aim high in steering. If you just fix your gaze right in front of your own car, and react to the brake lights only of the car right in front of you, a ten-car pileup is going to be the inevitable result.

No, you have to look way up the road. Is traffic up there slowing down? Do you see brake lights coming on on eight cars ahead? That's how you get your clue to slow down.

Is it possible to "aim high in steering" in our spiritual life? Can we focus our attention far up the road and become better defensive drivers on the highway toward the kingdom of God?

Think about a co-worker whose behavior at the office just burns you up. He comes in and criticizes your work. Boom! That's like brake lights flashing right in front of you. And the temptation is to react, to fight back, to rear-end him into submission.

But why not aim high? Will a quick jab back really solve things down the road? A week from now, will things be better or worse if you zing him right back? Won't an angry answer from you just make more traffic later?

Aim high! Think of a way to respond that will avoid a collision now and maybe even smooth things up for later. Wait a half hour, maybe . . . and then write a memo instead of screaming at him. Or take him to lunch and really talk over your grievance in a calm and constructive way.

Scenario number two. A temptation looms up ahead. Let's say you're a single Christian, and some casual sex is openly offered. Tonight! You can have him or her tonight! No strings attached.

But friend, aim high. Tonight might indeed be pretty special, pretty breathtaking. But what about up the road? What about a year from now, when this person has gone on to five other partners after you? What about two years from now when you're standing at the altar with your husband- or wife-to-be, wishing you had the gift of purity to give *then*? Do you get the idea?

Bear in mind that aiming high right now can even anticipate these problems. Back to that crabby co-worker. Look up the road and see that problem coming. You know he's going to be there first thing Monday. You know how he gets on your nerves. Prepare yourself ahead of time with prayer and a new attitude and maybe the cooperation of a trusted friend.

It's the same with that moment of sexual temptation. Admit it now—if you'd aimed your gaze a bit higher, you'd have seen that coming. In fact, maybe you even encouraged that dilemma, that traffic jam, with a bit of flirting or suggestion of your own. Aiming higher, you could have avoided that roadblock completely.

The Bible's full of stories of people who either did or didn't aim high. How about Esau, who sold his birthright, his entire spiritual blessing and inheritance, for a bowl of stew. Man, he was hungry *Right Now*! Never mind about next week or next year or the next 50 years! So he played "Let's Make a Deal" with his brother Jacob.

Or King David. There was Bathsheba, and she was beautiful. He had to have her now! Within the next half hour! And he didn't aim high long enough to see how his family and even his entire empire would be placed in jeopardy by one act of adultery.

Oh, but let's look at the good stories. How about Moses, who could have been Pharaoh "for a while," or God's champion for *eternity*? Or Abraham, who trusted God so much, he willingly started out on an open-ended journey, having no clear direction as to where he was going. These are men who aimed high in steering; they looked way up the road in following God's lead.

I get a thrill every time I read the verse in Hebrews that describes the mindset of Abraham and Isaac and Jacob. Chapter 11, the great Faith Chapter, verse 10: "For he [Abraham] was looking forward to the city with foundations, whose architect and builder is God."

Abraham didn't stop for every bump in the road, every detour or oasis along the way. He was aiming high in his steering; he had his eyes on a distant city called heaven. "Looking forward," the Bible says.

In fact, people like Abraham and Noah and Enoch and Moses had so learned to aim high in their earthly travels that they actually felt like strangers here. Verse 13 says: "They admitted that they were aliens and strangers on earth." Their gaze, their focus, was always on heaven.

And then, of course, there's Jesus in the Garden of Gethsemane. Tempted to take the short-term escape and just get out. And the devil screamed it in his ear: "Take off right now! You can catch the Thursday night red-eye flight out of this rebellious, ungrateful planet. Go on! You could be home by midnight tonight!" But Jesus aimed high. He looked up the road two thousand years and could sense how grateful you and I would be NOW for the gift of salvation. He saw you on the freeway way down here in these 1990s. He saw me. And so He stayed on the road to Calvary. He didn't turn away.

Friend, that's the driver's ed. philosophy we've got to have.

There was a missionary a few years ago named Helen Morton. *Doctor* Helen Morton, who decided to travel to the hill country of northern Thailand. Instead of making $500,000 a year here in California, she lived in a plain, makeshift, little village home with the natives and took long trips into the primitive countryside, healing and being a blessing. No luxury car, no swimming pool. On some of her trips, the only bathroom she could find would be a hole dug in the ground.

You had to wonder why she did it. And you especially had to wonder why when thieves came to her little house one day and attacked her. They shot and killed her right on her front porch. Even as you're reading these words, there's just a plain little white cross way out there on a hillside in Northern Thailand, ten thousand miles from home, with her name on it. "Helen Morton."

Why? Why give your life away like that? Why trade wealth for heartache?

Because Helen Morton aimed high in steering. Higher than a big paycheck. Higher than a big house. She looked higher and saw eternity and eternal life and the incomparable rewards of *service*, of seeing those hundreds of people she had helped to be saved in God's kingdom.

She looked way up the road and saw that city whose builder and maker is God.

CHAPTER 7

Get the Big Picture

Have you ever ridden from the airport to a rental car lot in one of those custom-built company vans? One with a huge blind spot because there isn't a rearview mirror? Perhaps you noticed that the driver actually has a television monitor with him right up front, so that a close-circuit TV camera can show him what's behind the van.

Now, that's really following our driver's ed. rule number 2: Get the big picture.

Some drivers only see the car that's right in front of them. That's it! If you're off to one side or three cars in front or behind them, you had better look out for yourself, because Mr. Blinders up there has no idea that you exist in his world. He just plain doesn't see you.

Maybe you've driven down a city street, or perhaps you were jogging, and a car approached from the side. And you could tell by looking that they didn't see you. They were looking in just one direction, and you were invisible to them.

If you've ever traveled in London, you know how hard it is as a pedestrian to "Get the big picture." We're so used to stepping off a curb after looking to the *left*! But in London cars are driving on the left, so they're coming at you from the right! And all the curbs have big arrows on them for dumb American visitors. "Look this way! Get the big picture."

In the spiritual realm, it's so important to do exactly that—Get the big picture! Try to get a grasp of the whole sweep of why we're here!

Many people live their entire lives without really pausing to consider that question. They're born, they live, and then they die. Life is just one quick roller coaster ride: fun in the sandbox, then elementary school, high school, college, a job and a spouse, two kids, vacation, a few moves, a few dollars in a Keough plan, retirement, and then those last moments fading into darkness. They never stop to say, "Is this it? Is there more? Is there a big picture that I just never saw?"

That's why I'm so grateful for a book called the Holy Bible. God's Word is the *one* Book, the one information source in the entire universe, that has the big picture, the whole story.

You know, a TV film or a history book can just paint the tiniest slice of the story. But it never tells it all. It can't fill in all the parts or explore the meaning behind the headlines and the plot lines. But the Bible has the whole picture, from beginning to end . . . and then even what comes *after* the end.

Genesis, chapter 1, of course, is the Creation story. *Our* beginning. And Revelation paints a picture of the end-time scenes. But in between those two boundary markers, we even find information that transcends this planet. You can read in the book of Job, chapter 1, a story of heavenly conflict, of debates between God and His ancient enemy. And in Isaiah, chapter 14, about Lucifer's ambitions, his secret desire to be like God. And then in Revelation, chapter 12, about war in heaven and Satan, the devil, the dragon, being cast down to this earth. And then over to chapter 20 of that same panoramic book, where the devil is both defeated and destroyed.

You know, all you can say is "Wow!" The Bible has it all! The big picture! Details from before this planet even began and more details that carry right on into a glorious future long after life on this earth comes to an end.

I want to encourage you right now to tap into that big picture. Think about this: a big picture is useless unless we're looking at it! A seventy-millimeter widescreen production is wasted unless you're watching and paying attention.

I remember Valerie Harper as "Rhoda," joking on the old *Mary Tyler Moore* show about her tiny little black-and-white five-inch television. The war movie *Tora Tora Tora* came on one night. And she complained to her friend, "On my screen, it just said 'Tora To . . .' " And that was it. She got half a movie.

So get into the Bible! Look for yourself and discover *God's big picture*. Get into a church fellowship where the pastoral staff and the congregation are wrestling with the grand sweep of history, of that big picture. Are they asking the three questions: "Where did I come from? What am I doing here? And where am I going?"

And then begin to apply that *big picture* to your own life. Does a knowledge of eternal things affect your daily decisions right here, today?

Consider this scene: a potential marital conflict. Something your spouse did has really hurt your feelings. And in your mind you play with two delicious options. One, you can lash back at him. Give it right back to him in his face! Double measure!

Or, option two, you can give him a good solid week of

silent treatment. Cold-shoulder him into submission. No conversation, no responses, no romance, no anything until he comes crawling.

But now, let's get the big picture. This man's been your husband for eighteen years. By and large, he's stood by you. He's been faithful. If you added up all the birthday cards and nice things he's done over the years, it's quite a pile. And now you've had this *one* fight.

Looking at the big picture, the big pile, is this latest mistake of his really worth one whole week of agony and revenge? Is it really worth it to stick the knife in and twist it? Sure, it might feel good right now. You've been practicing your mad little speech in the shower for the past two mornings; it'd feel so great to let him really have it. But is it worth it? All things considered, all things balanced out, is revenge really the best way?

And let me add something else. Put Calvary into your *big picture*. Jesus dying on the cross to save *you*, to forgive *you*. He put up with so much in order to rescue you from this very kind of wallowing in the mud.

Then ask yourself again. With this added to the *big picture*, is it worth it? Is fighting back really the best thing? Or could you actually participate in God's big picture by forgiving?

My writer friend Steven Mosley, in his recent book about temptation entitled *There I Go Again*, actually has a chapter entitled "The Big Picture." He describes World War Two prisoners in the Auschwitz death camp. Most of them were discouraged, beaten men and women. But a Viennese doctor, Viktor Frankl, noticed that a small group seemed to have a certain spark in their eyes. These were men who, riding back to camp in the darkness of a cattle truck after a freezing day at a worksite, would pause in the corner to pray together. These were men who managed to share their meager rations with the dying, to encourage a hopeless brother.

Somehow, Dr. Frankl discovered, these unique men had a kind of spiritual freedom which couldn't be taken away. They had a glimpse of a big picture, a reality that transcended the barbed-wire fences of Auschwitz. Their lives had meaning.

In fact, as he wrote later, these few men had—not a will-to-live or a will-to-power or a will-to-pleasure—but a *will-to-meaning*. They were determined that their lives would have meaning, that they were part of something bigger than their day-to-day fragile existences.

Just two pages later in his book, Mosley writes this: "We have a unique role to play on this planet which no one has had before in the history of the universe and no one else will again. We are called to reflect God's character in the midst of a world shattered by sin; we're called to embody truth in the place where it is distorted most horribly.

"Our growth in Christ can be driven by a will-to-meaning. Every time we are moved by the Spirit to express a part of the divine nature, Satan the accuser is intimidated, his alternative empire of sin is shown to be a sham, and the watching universe bears witness to the power of God to wrest beauty from the jaws of disaster."

Isn't that tremendous! You and I are part of something big. I suppose that's why, just about every week, it seems, this special verse pops up in our radio scripts. "Let your light so shine before men, that they may see your good works, and glorify your *Father* which is in heaven" (Matthew 5:16, KJV).

When you avoid that marital spat with your husband, when you obey some quiet command of God's, when you win even a small victory over the enemy, you participate in the *big picture* of God's ultimate victory. This is more than just today's little skirmish; you're a player in a global triumph.

I love the story of Noble Alexander, as told in the book *I Will Die Free*. This Seventh-day Adventist pastor survived twenty-two years in Castro's Cuban prison system. He underwent horrors that I simply can't describe to you—unbelievable tortures. But somehow he sensed that he was God's man in something far more important than just Cuban dungeons. He determined to live—and survive—for the purpose of being used by God. He would be God's man in that place. He would defeat his enemies by *living*—and by being faithful to God.

Today, Noble *is* a free man, serving as my fellow Adventist pastor here in America. Of course, for both of us, the wonderful promise of Jesus' soon coming is part of our Christian heritage. The hope of the second advent—Noble and I and so many others hold that as the greatest part of our *big picture*.

How about you?

CHAPTER 8

Keep Your Eyes Moving

They call it "highway hypnosis." You're on a long straight freeway like Interstate 5 here in California, or I-70 going through Kansas. And for 300 miles, it's just those two concrete ribbons of road going on and on and on.

After about five hours of that, you begin to enter zombieland. Unless you're playing the *Voice of Prophecy* on the radio, of course, you can really begin to glaze over. Your eyes lock in place, and a kind of hypnosis does take effect.

That's why rule number 3 from our driver's ed. instruction is so important: *Keep your eyes moving*. Every few seconds, in fact, you need to peek in the mirrors and check to the sides and look far up the road. Are cars merging onto the freeway right at the point where you zip by their on-ramp? Any potential conflict there? Is the car that's passing you right now going to move back across too quickly and clip your fender? When you're driving through town, is that kid playing ball in his yard suddenly going to jump in front of your car?

It's all part of "Getting the big picture," as we described in chapter 7.

I find this added rule to be especially helpful in the Christian life. Keep your eyes moving! Know what's happening around you! Be aware! Don't let a kind of "spiritual highway hypnosis" lead you into a fatal traffic accident.

This counsel is particularly apropos because you *know* there's an enemy out there, a freeway foe, determined to cause you problems. The Bible describes him in 1 Peter 5:8, and almost comes right out and says: "Keep your eyes moving." Notice: "Be controlled and alert." (No hypnosis here!) "Your enemy the devil prowls around like a roaring lion looking for someone to devour."

A lion in the zoo is one thing, isn't it? But if you're out in the jungle—and you hear a rumor that there's a lion out there in the jungle, too—I can promise that you'll have no problem keeping your eyes moving. Believe me, it'll come naturally then!

Maybe you remember this King James rendition of Peter's warning: "Be sober, be vigilant." God is warning us to keep our eyes moving, to stay on the lookout. Check your mirrors; glance over to the side. Most of all, stay awake!

Of course, when we say, "Stay awake," we can't help but think again of that Thursday evening in the Garden of Gethsemane. For some hard-to-understand reason, Peter and James and John simply could not stay awake! They were drowsy; they were exhausted. Even when Jesus begged them to stay awake with Him—and told them that He needed them—their eyes simply wouldn't stay open.

But maybe it's not so surprising. Remember, we have an enemy who loves the sound of snoring. He loves to see us asleep. He fills the air with hypnotic suggestions, sweet whispers, that lull us into such a comfortable slumber.

Keep Your Eyes Moving

No wonder Jesus said to His disciples: "Watch and pray so that you will not fall into temptation. The spirit is willing, but the body is weak" (Mark 14:37).

Jesus knew full well what temptations were right in front of them, just hours away. He knew that Peter would face three temptations that very night—the temptations to deny his Lord. "Watch and pray," He implored Peter. "Keep your eyes open! Keep them moving! The enemy's very near."

You know, over in the book of Luke we can find this same "watch and pray" theme again. Not only in chapter 22, the Garden of Gethsemane scene, but also in chapter 21, where Jesus is describing to His disciples the temptations and trials of the last days of earth's history. He paints a word picture for them, outlining the signs of the end: false christs, earthquakes, wars, persecution. And then comes the same warning, intended for those of us living in these 1990s.

Here it is again in verse 36: "Be always on the watch, and pray that you may be able to escape all that is about to happen, and that you may be able to stand before the Son of Man."

Friend, that's a heavenly driver's ed. warning with your name on it and mine. We're alive *now*—in the very time Christ was speaking of. We're in the very last days of earth's history, and Jesus Christ is saying to us right now: "Lonnie, David, stay awake! Keep your eyes moving! Look around you! Pray more than you've ever prayed before!" And the same message is for you, as well.

If you're a parent, keep your eyes moving on behalf of your children. Do you have a sense for how many times television blind-sides our kids with sin? You're watching something that you think is acceptable and noble—and then, *BOOM!* A commercial or a stay-tuned-for-this-next-show promo comes on, and it's loaded with Satan's spectacular traps. And you had no idea that little bomb was coming into your house. No wonder Jesus says, "Keep your eyes moving."

And in our own lives—there are some places we as Christians simply shouldn't go! Are your eyes moving so that you'll know what to avoid? Some stores we just don't belong in. There are some kinds of entertainment where God's people don't belong. There are some things on television and on those airplane movie screens that we shouldn't see. In those cases, we need to keep our eyes moving in another direction.

But the point here is this: know where those traps are so that you can steer well away from them—just like a good driver who spots a big pothole way up the road and is able to completely avoid it.

I find some other lessons in these four words: "Keep your eyes moving." There are some people whose eyes just naturally move to spot those who are hurting. Are you one of those? If somebody's in the hospital . . . somehow they're the first to find out and get a card and send flowers. If a person's going through a divorce, they're already on their way to share a comforting hug. Is there a funeral? This person has noticed the announcement and made plans to attend—or write a personal note if it's clear across the country.

What a beautiful way to "Keep your eyes moving"!

But there's another pointed little application that maybe we could all benefit from. It's so easy in this life to get hold of one idea and just get fixated on that *one* cause to the point of losing your way. You can aim down one freeway so intensely, so fiercely, that you just can't see that the road is going off a cliff.

I've received publications in the mail from people who decided that pornography was *their* issue. Now, let me say this: pornography is an evil thing. I praise God for people who are being used by heaven to fight it.

But some people enter into such a crusade mentality just over pornography that they forget to be kind and Christlike in their behavior. I've read magazines that were filled from the front cover to the back page with antipornography hate. Inside the magazine, you could read vivid, colorful descriptions of all the worst TV shows and films. I mean, these lewd accounts were almost worse than the programs themselves . . . and here all the sin was condensed into thirty-two breathless, angry pages.

And I've said to myself, "You know, these people are forgetting to keep their eyes moving. Perhaps they need to move away from their late-night TV screens and spend some time in Sabbath School or Sunday school focusing again on the purity and quiet strength of Jesus Christ."

Again, please don't misunderstand. A campaign against pornography is a good thing. To be a soldier in the trenches in combatting child abuse or corruption or abortion is a noble thing. But "Keep your eyes moving." Allow Jesus Christ to always be in your vision.

Here at the *Voice of Prophecy*, we were blessed for so many years to be led by "The Chief"—Pastor H. M. S. Richards. Many hundreds of you reading these words remember him well, I know. What a godly man!

And Pastor Richards really had just one theme in his life. One theme that was two words long. And whenever anyone asked him, "Brother Richards, what's the message?" he would reply, "Jesus only. Jesus only." I guess he was a lot like the Apostle Paul, who in 1 Corinthians, chapter 2, said this: "For I resolved to know nothing while I was with you except Jesus Christ and Him crucified."

Pastor Richards was a great preacher, inventive in his use of radio back in the 1930s. He was brilliant at keeping his eyes moving and finding contemporary illustrations. But his gaze always came back to his Saviour: "Jesus only." And we'd all have to admit that he did a pretty good job of driving, navigating, in his spiritual journey toward the kingdom of God.

Finally, let me remind you to let your eyes go to the rearview mirror once in a while. Look behind you and see how God has blessed you and saved you and guided you in the past.

One of the pioneers in my own Adventist denomination once wrote these beautiful words of encouragement: "In reviewing our past history, having traveled over every step of advance to our present standing, I can say, Praise God! As I see what the Lord has wrought, I am filled with astonishment, and with confidence in Christ as leader. We have nothing to fear for the future, except as we shall forget the way the Lord has led us."—Ellen White, *Life Sketches*, 196.

Yes, keep your eyes moving, and look behind you on occasion . . . but keep them *focused* on the future we have in Jesus Christ.

CHAPTER 9

Make Sure Others See You

Have you ever noticed that a car horn can sound mean . . . or friendly? And I suppose most of us have been on the receiving end of both kinds.

Some people's horns will almost knock you right through the windshield. If a traffic light turns from red to green and you don't get off the line within the first one-third of a second, boy, someone behind you lets you have it with all 900 decibels.

But then there's the friendly *tap* on a horn where someone driving by just wants to say Hi. Or the kind of little honk that simply says in a helpful way, "I'm here. Please watch out."

What are the spiritual applications we can find in your car's horn? Rule number 4 in our driver's ed. list is a simple one, just five words long: Make sure others see you.

Defensive driving, you remember, operates on the assumption that everybody else on the road *isn't* looking out for you. They're paying attention to their own driving dilemmas, stewing over their own mother-in-law problems, and tuning in their own favorite radio station as they drive. They're not looking for you, so you have to make sure that they see you're there.

Perhaps you recall that old driver's ed. film where the driving instructor demonstrated little tricks that could make sure others notice where you are on the road and what your intentions are. Your turn signals, for example. Using them faithfully gives everyone on the road a clear idea about where you're heading. Everyone knows your destination.

And—your horn! Your *friendly* horn.

Let's say you're driving down a residential area, and you see a mother who's just loaded her three children into the family car. She climbs in behind the wheel, and you see her backup lights go on. She has no idea that you're coming down the street.

So you give her a friendly little tap on the horn, just as a polite way of saying, "Ma'am, I want you to notice that I'm here. Those are three lovely kids with you in the car, and I really don't want to run into you folks. That's all." And she hears that little *beep*, so she waits.

You may be thinking, "OK, Pastor Lonnie, now we're going to move to the Christian application. And a slogan like 'Make sure others see you' seems like the exact opposite of what Christians should be trying to do!"

In a way, you're right! We think immediately about that Pharisee standing in the temple with his long and boastful prayer. Or the religious rich of Jesus' day who gave huge offerings and hired a brass band and a Jerusalem PR agency to announce their generous moment.

Yes, in Matthew, chapter 6, Jesus said things like: "Let your giving be done in secret. Don't even let your left hand know how much your right hand is giving. And let your praying be done in secret too. Go into the closet and say your prayers."

At the same time, Jesus was aware that people were always watching Him. And that they're always going to be watching His followers. If you're a believer, people are watching you right now. And what is it they're seeing?

As humble and emptied of self as Jesus Christ was, He had a very clear understanding of what we might call global public relations. Do you remember this verse in John 12, where He says to His followers, in speaking of the crucifixion: "But I, when I am lifted up from the earth, will draw all men to myself" (verse 32).

Have you ever asked yourself why Jesus allowed Himself to be the object of attention during that triumphal procession just days before the events at Calvary? Why would the humble Saviour permit the disciples to place Him on a donkey and parade Him through the streets and accept the adoring praise of the crowds until the priests and rulers came running out to protest?

Jesus knew full well that the event coming up, His sacrifice on the cross, was to be the turning point of all history. And this gift was something He and all heaven wanted the world, and even the universe, to notice.

There was nothing prideful or self-exalting about Christ's motives. But He knew the world needed to see the incredible love of God poured out in that Friday-afternoon gift on Calvary. He wanted the world to know.

And in a humble, God-glorifying way, I believe it's acceptable and even *good* for you to obey the driver's ed. rule and "Make sure others see God in you." Remember Matthew 5:16? "Let your light so shine before men that they may see your good works and glorify your *Father* which is in heaven" (KJV).

An October 17, 1994, citizen-editorial in *Newsweek* magazine's "My Turn" column was entitled "Mind Your

Tongue, Young Man." Sandra Maurer, of Grand View College in Des Moines, writes about being in a convenience store behind a young man wanting to buy a Pepsi and a pack of cigarettes.

When the clerk requested ID for the cigarettes, the kid exploded in an expletive-laced tirade. He didn't have the stupid ID with him! He didn't carry it everywhere he went, for heaven's sake!

"No ID, no cigarettes," the clerk said firmly.

Then the fireworks really began as the teenager began to scream out a torrent of obscene filth. All at once, the clerk reached across the counter with both arms, picked up the kid by the collar, and lifted him right off the ground. "That's enough!" he snapped. "You watch what you say in here. There's a lady present!"

And Sandra Maurer writes: "Instinctively, I looked around to see where the 'lady' was. I had an image of some little old woman in a housedress, shuffling along in sturdy orthopedic shoes, her white hair done up in a bun, her purse dangling from her arm. I didn't see her anywhere."

All of a sudden, she looked in the convenience store mirror and realized . . . the "lady" was her! That tough, strong clerk was speaking out on her behalf! He had noticed her and had moved in to provide protection.

A group of men were sitting together having a conversation one day when one of them remembered a favorite little joke. "I guess there aren't any ladies around," he said by means of a preamble, glancing around and lowering his voice as people sometimes do when they're about to launch into an R-rated story.

There was a moment of pause. Then one of the men slowly stood up. "No . . . but there's a gentleman." And he left. No screaming, no puritanical sermon, not even a tone of condemnation. But he graciously tapped on the horn, so to speak, as if to say, "Guys, I'm here. Take notice that a man of purity and principle is in your presence. And now I must leave."

It can be a beautiful thing when quiet, gracious Christians are in the room—and people *know* they're in the room. When Christians, whose sole desire in life is to bring honor to God, quietly clear their throats and say, "Listen, I'm here. And I stand for the King of the Universe."

Here at the *Voice of Prophecy*, we're not heavily into PR. We don't have any fan clubs or billboards. But I will say this: We don't go on the radio *not* to be heard.

I'm glad that you've found this book and that maybe you've discovered our daily program. Not because I want the name Melashenko to become a household word or to get an invitation to a White House prayer breakfast. I want this radio ministry to be noticed because our *Voice of Prophecy* staff has dedicated itself to sharing Jesus Christ in attractive and compelling and scriptural ways fifty-two weeks a year.

The title of a wonderful book written about ten years ago by Rebecca Pippert says it all: *Out of the Saltshaker and Into the World*. Salt, in order to be effective, has to get out of the shaker and into the food, permeating every bite with its flavor.

How is it for you? Do your co-workers know that you're Christ's ambassador there at the office? Do your neighbors see you living out the life of Jesus there on your cul-de-sac? Is your friendly horn beeping in your community, letting people know that the Holy Spirit is working in *your* life?

A few years ago, pop star Bonnie Raitt sang a song that basically said what we're saying right here. "People are watching. They're looking at us. They see how we look at one another; they listen in on our conversations." Her song, of course, takes a romantic turn, when she concludes: "Let's give them something to talk about. How about love?"

You know, Christians might do well to take that same advice. "Let's give them something to talk about."

CHAPTER 10

Leave Yourself an Out

Have you ever heard of the "Three-Second Rule?" It's one that good drivers over the years have made their motto when trying to follow at a safe distance behind another car.

When you're on the freeway, you watch as the car in front of you passes some landmark or road sign. Then you simply count—"Leviticus ONE, Leviticus TWO, Leviticus THREE"—and make sure that you don't pass that same landmark before three seconds have elapsed. That way, regardless of what speed you're traveling, you have a full three seconds of reaction time in order to escape from a jam.

Our driver's ed. rule number 5, which is a cousin of the Three-Second Rule, goes like this: "Leave yourself an out."

At all times on the highway, you should *know* what you would do if a crisis loomed. Is there space to the side? Could you hit the brakes—or is there a truck right behind you?

Leave Yourself an Out

That offramp up ahead . . . could you use that as an escape hatch?

Now obviously, when you're driving out in the wide-open spaces, you don't need to have this slogan, "Leave yourself an out," pounding in your head through the whole trip. But when you're in traffic, it's a good idea to always know what you would do to avoid trouble.

And what about during our drive toward the City of God? As we travel in all this congestion down the highway of life, is this a good slogan to remember: "Leave Yourself an Out"?

You may be thinking at this very moment: "Lonnie, you don't know where I am. I'm on a collision course . . . and there is no way out! No way!" Right now, you might see a spiritual head-on collision coming, and you're hemmed in. There's nowhere to turn.

Did you know the Bible addresses that very situation? In Paul's first letter to the believers in Corinth, in chapter 10, verse 12, he talks about the tendency to glide down the road thinking everything is fine. "So, if you think you are standing firm, be careful that you don't fall!"

All right. That's warning number 1. If you're gliding along at 65 miles an hour and everything looks good, be careful! Keep your eyes moving! Danger—a slippery spot—may be coming up.

But now the good news about collisions. Verse 13: "No temptation has seized you except what is common to man," Paul writes. "And God is faithful; He will not let you be tempted beyond what you can bear. But when you are tempted, He will also provide a way out so that you can stand up under it."

In the King James rendition, we're promised that God will provide "a way of escape" for us. There *is* a way out of every temptation, every trap. You might feel overwhelmed, but this is God's promise.

Now, let's be very open with each other. I know how easy

it is to drop a Bible verse into a book chapter—or cheerfully read it over the radio. And you've got to be thinking to yourself: "Listen, Melashenko. I'm telling you—you don't know my circumstances! You don't know how tough things are for me!"

You're absolutely right. But in my many years in the ministry, I've experienced firsthand and in the lives of my many parishioners God's fulfillment of this promise. There *is* a way of escape from every spiritual dilemma if we're willing to take it.

Maybe you're caught in the trap of holding onto a grudge. You've hated a certain someone for so many months now, you don't see any way to let it go. And every Sunday in church, there they are, singing in the choir. Pretending that everything is fine, when you know how they've cheated you. The temptation to keep despising that person is so overwhelming, you're sure there's no way out. You can't get past it!

But listen. I've known people in those very circumstances . . . and yet, they finally came to understand that the Christian concept of *forgiveness* meant simply handing their emotions and their hatred and their desire for revenge to God and saying, "Lord, take this! You take it! If this person needs punishing, I trust You to do it. You're a big enough God to handle this for me."

I've seen people actually hand their desire for revenge over to God, just like it was a suitcase bulging with dirty laundry. And then they were FREE! They'd been given a way of escape from that very temptation! It worked!

What about those moments of crisis, of quick and sudden temptation? Where is our "out" at times like that?

Well, our best example is always Jesus. Three times in Matthew 4, Christ was hit by the devil with megavoltage temptations. Overpowering! Tempted with food after He'd been without for forty days and nights. Tempted to put Himself on display in order to attract attention. Tempted to take a shortcut—a ten-second pretend-to-worship-the-devil detour—that would spare Him the entire ordeal of Calvary.

Let me ask you: are those temptations somehow easier than yours? Did Jesus get off light? Friend, He faced three blockbusters in a row . . . the kinds of temptations where you and I might concede: "OK, there's no way out. There's no escape. Not this time."

And yet Jesus *did* have an out. Three times in a row, He found His escape. Three times in a row, He used the same three words: "It is written." The promises of the Bible were His refuge. He took Satan's misquotations of the Bible and threw them right back in his face.

I can remember driving through some of those vicious hills in Colorado on I-70; long, steep hills up—and then really long five-mile rides straight down the other side. It's something like the grapevine on I-5 here in southern California.

And if you ever lost your brakes on one of those long downhill stretches, especially in a semi or a huge 18-wheeler, you'd have no chance. None! There'd be no way to steer safely to the bottom. No matter how smart a driver you are, the law of physics would defeat you.

Except for one thing. The roadbuilders have strategically placed escape routes: "Runaway Lanes," they call them. Have you seen them? They're made out of gravel, and right when you might need one most, there it is. It veers off to the right and then goes sharply uphill to stop a runaway truck.

Friend, there *is* a way of escape. For every temptation, there is a way out. God's promised to provide it.

You know, God is so good. He's the Master of everything; He provides for our every need. And if we're in "quick trouble," an unexpected challenge, we're told that we can call on Him anytime. Psalm 4:3 is just one of hundreds of passages where we're given this assurance by King David: "The Lord will hear when I call to him."

That's good news. Still, how much better it is to drive in such a way that sudden escape lanes aren't needed!

We've mentioned in these chapters driver's ed. principles including "Aim high in steering," "Get the big picture," and "Keep your eyes moving." When the Christian does that, then it isn't as necessary to swerve off the freeway with your brakes squealing in order to avoid an accident.

And by keeping our eyes moving, we can be prepared when the moment of crisis does come.

Let's consider again the triumph of Jesus when He was bombarded with those three temptations. Three times in a row Christ was able to quote Scripture, to call on Bible promises in order to defeat His enemy.

Did He have a copy of the Bible right there with Him? Was He able to say to His adversary: "Hold that thought! Let me look for a verse"?

No, Christ came to the battle already fortified! He went to the desert knowing He was going to be tempted, and He had already prepared Himself. He had filled His mind with God's Word *beforehand*. He was ready for the crisis before the crisis came.

The time for you and me to read our Bibles is *now*! The time to learn to trust in God is *now*! Are you gliding along the freeway in pretty good shape right now? Praise God for His blessings . . . and use this peaceful time to prepare for tomorrow's temptations. Aim high in steering, keep your eyes moving, and get ready.

In my years of pastoring, I've had one special bit of advice to share with the teenagers in my church families. You and I both know the kinds of temptations they can face, especially in the areas of dating and sex and drugs and peer pressure. And I say to them: "Have your 'no' ready. Right now while things are calm and you're thinking clearly. Don't wait until someone's pressuring you for an answer: 'Come on, baby, how about it?' Get your 'no' ready now!"

"Leave yourself an out."

People going through a Twelve-step program often plan to have a person they can call when a critical temptation lands on their doorstep. Have that phone number ready ahead of time.

"Leave yourself an out."

With the "Promise Keepers" movement that's currently sweeping the country, thousands of Christian men are bonding with one another, holding each other accountable as godly fathers and sexually pure husbands. They call each other to give encouragement and to leave themselves an out.

It's a tough drive. There are a lot of drive-by shootings on this highway. Quite a few accidents. But God's promised us a successful journey. We're going to make it all the way home. And I'm glad you and I are driving in the same direction.

SECTION 3

Being a Part of the Team

CHAPTER 11

The Woman Who Picks Up the Rice

Eleanor was a member of a "superchurch." There were several thousand members, and every Sunday morning she sat alone in the corner of the same pew, quietly listening to the sermon. She looked around her each week; there were deacons and elders and Sunday school teachers and visitation coordinators and the woman who organized the schedule for people to sponsor the floral arrangements. Just about everyone seemed to have a function to fulfill except for her. She didn't seem to feel very needed or important.

She knew that her small financial contributions each month, her tithes, were such a tiny little dribble in a vast river of giving. It didn't really count for much. Maybe she didn't count for much either. She was just one of the quiet, lonely people who seem to be in every church.

I have to confess that Eleanor is kind of a fictional character. I borrowed her from an old ballad dating back to the 1960s entitled *Eleanor Rigby* by a group you may have heard of—John, Paul, George, and Ringo. Between all the "I Want to Hold Your Hand"s and "Yeah Yeah Yeah"s from the Beatles came this one quiet, almost spiritual message. Maybe you remember these sad lines while the violins played: "Eleanor Rigby, picks up the rice in the church where the wedding has been. Lives in a dream."

And then in the third verse it says this: "Eleanor Rigby, died in the church and was buried along with her name. Nobody came."

The song goes on to ask, where do all the lonely people come from? Where do they all belong?

There are so many people *in the church* who feel like Eleanor Rigby. They don't seem to have a part to play. Their meager offerings don't buy them a vote or a seat or a voice on the church board. They don't have any talents, it seems, so it's actually a relief when the nominating committee passes them over every year. About all they're good for is to pick up the rice in the church where the wedding has been.

First Corinthians 12 has something to say about all the Eleanor Rigbys in the church. This is the often-read "body of Christ" chapter, where the apostle Paul challenges the Christian church with the realization that we as believers are one complete body, made up of many important parts. Notice verse 12: "The body is a unit, though it is made up of many parts; and though all its parts are many, they form one body."

I think that's an important realization—often lost sight of. Eleanor Rigby is a part of something; in fact, something much larger than that one church she attended. As a Christian, all the Eleanors of the world are parts—body parts—if you will, in a global, even universal, two-thousand-year-old alive and functioning thing called the body of Christ.

And there is *no such thing* as an unimportant body part!

The Woman Who Picks Up the Rice

Maybe you remember a classic old book coming out of the 1910s entitled *Cheaper By the Dozen*. Frank Gilbreth and his wife, Lillie, decided that they were going to have twelve kids. In fact, on their wedding day, as they got on the steam-engine train to head out for their honeymoon, they talked about it and shook hands on their agreement to have six boys and six girls. Certainly things like dolls and baseball bats and roller skates would come "cheaper by the dozen."

Well, it's a clever, funny book, and sure enough, they had exactly twelve kids. Wouldn't you know it, it came out six boys and six girls. Just about every year, through a span of seventeen years, every time Mr. Gilbreth whistled assembly to show off his tribe to visitors, he'd be able to get right down to the end and then hold up the baby and say, "And here's the latest model." Or, "We're expecting the latest model sometime in February," an announcement which always embarrassed his wife.

One of the tongue-in-cheek points of humor was always that with that many kids, you could hardly keep track of how many there were. "How many is it now, Lillie?" he'd ask his wife. "Nine? Ten? I can't remember." Implying that if you lost one or two here and there out of a dozen, well, it wouldn't be any big deal.

Even the kids would sometimes cash in on that kind of humor. On Saturday nights, the Gilbreth children would put on little dramas for their parents, an audience of two, and mimic their own dad, who was a motion-study expert. They'd stage a "pretend" visit to a sawmill, and one of the children, playing the part of a foreman, would gasp, "Tell your kids to get away from that saw! They'll get killed!"

"Oh, that's how they learn," the pretend Mr. Gilbreth would say casually.

"But he's squatting over that buzz saw!"

"The little rascal thinks it's a bicycle. Leave him alone."

Then someone offstage would give out a dying scream and the kid playing the part of Frank Gilbreth would kind of shrug and say, "Oh, well. The rest of you kids stay away from that saw now, you hear?" And then he'd add, "Somebody make a note of how many places we should set for supper."

But I want to tell you something. In real life, you better believe that the real Mr. Frank Gilbreth loved every single one of those twelve kids. There wasn't one who was expendable. There wasn't one whom you could just leave by the side of the road and then drive off with the others in "Foolish Carriage," the family's old Pierce Arrow. Every child, every part of that Gilbreth "body," that family, was worth inestimable millions.

In fact, one summer Gilbreth tacked up on the wall a piece of graph paper that was a thousand squares wide and a thousand squares high: a million squares. "That's one million right there, kids," he told them. "Some people have a million dollars; and that's how many it is."

Little Billy spoke up and said, "Do you have a million dollars, Daddy?"

"No," Dad said, kind of wistfully. "I have a million kids instead. Somewhere in life a man has to choose between the two."

But you know, there's a quiet lesson in this old story of a man whose every child was so precious. All through the book you read about Anne, Ernestine, Martha, Frank, Bill, Lill, Fred, Dan, Jack, Bob, and Jane. And unless you stop and count, you don't really realize that that's only eleven kids.

You have to read the book very, very carefully to discover that a girl named Mary was born between Anne and Ernestine. She's never mentioned except very briefly on two pages, and you have to read between the lines and figure that she must have died very early in life.

And for some reason, Frank, Jr. and Ernestine, the two Gilbreth children who wrote *Cheaper by the Dozen*, just couldn't bring themselves to write about Mary. The pain must have been so great for this family, that in a book filled with laughter and fun, they simply could not bring Mary back into the story. So all through the pages of adventure, it's Anne, Ernestine, Martha, Frank, Bill, Lill, Fred, Dan, Jack, Bob, Jane. And Mary, that precious twelfth child, remained a private secret, a hidden treasure for the Gilbreth family.

I find in this sweet story confirmation of a beautiful Bible verse found in 1 Corinthians 12:22. "And some of the parts that seem weakest and least important are really the most necessary" (*The Living Bible*).

In terms of lifespan and achievements and headlines, little Mary Gilbreth could likely be classed as "weakest," or "least important." But not to that Gilbreth family! In the book, a small part, a single line. But in their hearts, she was surely deemed as being "most necessary." She was a part of that family; she was part of that precious dozen.

In a wonderful 1992 book entitled *The Body*, Chuck Colson and Ellen Santilli Vaughn explore the Greek concept of *koinonia*. Is religion just a hot-tub experience? they ask. A phenomenon where people gather to "spend time together" at a weekend retreat or on the beach at Waikiki? Coming together for lunch at the "fellowship hall"? Is that all fellowship is?

"But the word for fellowship in the New Testament Greek, *koinonia*, means none of these; it is something much richer. Literally it means a communion, a participation of people together in God's grace. It describes a new community in which individuals willingly covenant to share in common, to be in submission to each other, to support one another and to 'bear one another's burdens,' as Paul wrote to the Galatians, and to build each other up in relationship with the Lord."

I find inherent in these powerful words the pillar of truth that *every person* in that communion is important and vital. This "new community" brings people together, values each person, loves each person, supports each person, shares grace with each person.

Even Eleanor Rigby, whose contribution was to pick up the rice after the wedding, ought to be a part of this communion. What she does counts! And when she dies, the church ought to be filled. The whole body of Christ should be there.

CHAPTER 12

Don Knotts Gets a Date

I'm not about to play Siskel and Ebert on our *Voice of Prophecy* broadcasts or in this book, but I do want to refer you to an old, kind of whimsical, Halloween comedy entitled *The Ghost and Mr. Chicken*. Don Knotts, all 98 pounds of him, is the hero . . . and, of course, he's made a pretty decent Hollywood living for decades playing a lovable, sweet, very nerdy, very wimpy kind of guy, a "Barney Fife." Always taking karate lessons by mail—that kind of thing.

In this old film, "Luther" is trying to win the heart of a girl much prettier than you'd expect he could ever get. But amazingly enough, "Alma" actually kind of seems to like Luther. And one evening, she cooks him a good supper, and they end up sitting together on the porch swing.

He's got to say something romantic to her, so after several minutes of awkward stammering and stuttering around, this memorable little pitch comes out. "Alma," he says, "you're a real attractive girl. Way above average."

"Oh. Well, thank you," she says.

He goes on. "Now I'm your average guy. Just average." She waits. And then he comes up with the line I've never forgotten. He takes a deep breath and says, " 'Average' is just plain lucky to be sitting on the same porch with 'above average.' "

And you know, that's really the cry of so many people in the church today. "I'm just average," we say. "Maybe even below average. In our church, I'm the 'Don Knotts' of the entire congregation. No talents. No abilities. No dazzling looks, no operatic singing voice for the choir. The Body of Christ really doesn't need me."

But 1 Corinthians 12 beautifully refutes such thinking! If you feel small and insignificant, like you're just playing a bit part, then these verses are specifically for you. Notice: "If the foot should say, 'Because I am not a hand, I do not belong to the body,' it would not for that reason cease to be part of the body. And if the ear should say, 'Because I am not an eye, I do not belong to the body,' it would not for that reason cease to be part of the body" (15, 16).

I suppose for most of us, it would be natural to consider a hand to be more important, more useful, than a foot. A hand probably plays a more active role; it's out front, while your feet, a lot of the time, are tucked under your desk at work where no one can see them. But would you want to try to get along without those two feet of yours? A lot of us have had to try, just for a very temporary time, and were we ever glad when the bandages came off or the cast was removed.

Do you remember ever hearing about an insignificant little device called an "O ring"? Just a plain, no-glamour gizmo—no big deal. But you can bet that a space shuttle never goes up into space without a very high-paid engineer checking those "O rings." When the space shuttle *Challenger* tragedy took place—it was those little "O rings" that didn't function right. What could a body do without the little parts, the little people?

Don Knotts Gets a Date

The apostle Paul goes on with some very keen observations. True, the eye is probably a more glamorous sense organ than the ear. But notice this: "If the whole body were an eye, where would the sense of hearing be? If the whole body were an ear, where would the sense of smell be? But, in fact, God has arranged the parts in the body, every one of them, just as He wanted them to be. If they were all one part, where would the body be? As it is, there are many parts, but one body" (17-20).

Paul almost slips up and shows us his sense of humor here, doesn't he? The whole body being an eye? Or an ear? That's quite a visual image. But you know, that's really what many people expect the Church to be. Everyone should be able to preach, they say. Or teach the lesson. Or get up in front and have exceptional people skills.

But as I mentioned in the last chapter, we also need the Eleanor Rigbys in our church. The quiet woman who faithfully picks up the rice in the church where the wedding has been. She can't lead out in a women's retreat or mastermind this year's fundraising drive to buy new carpeting for the fellowship hall. She's not articulate enough to fill in for the pastor on Sabbath morning.

But she has that unglamorous yet oh-so-necessary gift of *service*. She picks up the rice. She helps clean up after a potluck. She drives senior citizens to the grocery store. And the apostle Paul says so eloquently: "Where would we be without Eleanor Rigby? Without Don Knotts? Without Plain Jane and Average Andy?"

All through the Bible, God's Word makes it plain that even those who do the small things—*they count!* Their small, ordinary, unnoticed accomplishments count for the kingdom of God.

A mother packs a lunch for her small son. Five little loaves and two fishes. Now, that's not a big act; it's not a headline-maker. We don't know the little boy's name; we don't know the mother's name. But this is one of the most loved, often-told stories in the Bible.

A woman named Mary, a nobody—in fact, a recovering prostitute—buys a bottle of perfume and pours it over the head of Jesus. Have you ever heard that story before? Of course you have. We all have. In fact, Jesus revealed to His disciples that this story would be told everywhere around the world where the gospel was shared.

A woman puts her last two coins in the offering plate. It's a little offering given by one of the little people, one of the nobodies of the world. But Jesus looks at that quiet moment of sacrifice and He tells His disciples just how important, how precious, how meaningful, how substantial in the eyes of God in heaven that gift truly is. And if you were to add up all the sermons preached and all the books written and all the millions given because of those two little coins, you'd have to agree that this woman's gift counted.

Let me challenge not only your thinking right now, but perhaps your lifestyle. Move away from the thought, "I'm nothing . . . and my gifts and talents are nothing too." Move away from that! If you're a Christian today, then you're a Christian for a reason. God intervened and brought you into His family for a reason. Not just because He loves you, but also because He *needs* you. You have something that He can't get from any other place. You have a talent to use, an ability to share, a gift to exercise. In terms of human opinions and this world's yardsticks, it may not be a glamour gift. You may be a body part no one ever sees or notices. But God gave you that talent for the purpose of serving.

But let me pile on a second thought. Don't think of your gifts as being small—at the same time, don't be satisfied with small. There's legitimacy to your little, but you might well be able to do more than a little, maybe even a lot more. Maybe you're using one talent for the Lord when you could be using two or three or five for Him.

Don Knotts Gets a Date

You remember the Bible story, I'm sure, where a master gave one man a single, solitary talent. But there was another man who was given five! That man could do more, and the master expected more. Perhaps you've been giving a half hour a week to serve your local church. That's wonderful, and I praise God for your spirit of service. But could you be giving more time? Perhaps much more? Are you maybe giving small financial contributions when you could give much more? Are you participating by being present just occasionally, when really, you could be there seated in your pew every single weekend?

It's a powerful Bible truth that the body, the church of Christ, really needs every single one of us to participate—*and* to do what we can. In that early church we read about in Matthew, Mark, Luke, and John, there was the woman who put in two cents. What a part she played! On the other hand, there were Nicodemus and Joseph of Arimathea, both of them fabulously wealthy and influential. They were the first two millionaires in the Christian faith! What a failure it would have been if *they* had just put in two cents. They were abundantly blessed, and they gave service in like measure.

Let's return now to our porch where Don Knotts is sitting there with Alma. And he says to her, " 'Average' is just plain lucky to be sitting on the same porch with 'above average.' " In a sense, we who are Christians should say that every single day. Jesus our Saviour loves us. Extraordinary Saviour—Average us! It's an amazing thought, an incredible discovery. Do we deserve to sit on the same porch with Him, to work in His service, to be a part of His body? Of course we don't! It's the mismatched romance of all time! "Beauty and the Beast"! But He's invited us up onto that porch. "Sit with Me," He says. "Work with Me. I love you; I need you."

I know that Don Knotts, there on that porch with Alma, all tongue-tied and excited—he gave that relationship everything he had. Friend, how about me . . . and you?

CHAPTER 13

Brought to L.A. for One At-bat

In September of 1995, a great tragedy struck here in the Los Angeles area. Our beloved L.A. Dodgers were playing in Philadelphia, when a pitcher named Jeff Juden came up with the bases loaded and hit a home run, a grand slam, against the Dodgers. A pitcher!

As all of you baseball fans know, that is simply not acceptable behavior. First of all, pitchers don't hit homers. They should never be allowed to hit grand-slam homers, and especially not against the Los Angeles Dodgers, the unofficial favorite team of the *Voice of Prophecy*. (Except for the one loud-mouthed New Yorker on our staff.)

But that unexpected home run by a pitcher is somewhat applicable to the message of 1 Corinthians, chapter 12—at least, we're trying to salvage something good from the situation. According to Paul, every single person, every team member, if you will, has a part to play. Every role is important; every person on the roster has something unique that only they can contribute.

As this Bible passage certainly concedes, some parts get more attention and notice than others. I'm sure that former major leaguers pass away every single week of the year; most of them don't get mentioned. When someone named Mickey Mantle dies, however, it's a front-page story. Everyone hears about it. Some players are more famous than other players.

And yet, there's a certain rule that's both a baseball rule and a Bible rule. *Sooner or later, YOUR moment comes.* The day comes when your unique contribution is needed. The game comes when even that pitcher's swing of the bat is crucial; the team needs that grand slam.

Probably the most memorable line, the sound-bite verse from the entire book of Esther, all ten chapters, is found back in chapter 4. Esther, just a regular Jewish girl, a commoner, has been made queen. God had directed events and overruled in the affairs of mankind so that His chosen person, this young woman, is the new queen of Persia.

And now the children of Israel are in deep trouble. They're facing certain death because of an imperial decree. Only Queen Esther has it in her power to say a word to the king. It's all in her lap, so to speak. But there's risk to her if she gets involved. And as she's weighing her options, she gets a message from Mordecai, her adoptive father, who says to her: "Who knows whether you have come to the kingdom for such a time as this?" (verse 14).

What a marvelous sermon that is! What an unforgettable line! "Queen Esther—little Jewish girl—all your life you've been waiting. And now your time has come. This is the moment you've been preparing for."

Everything else Queen Esther had done up to that point—attending banquets, being a part of the palace retinue, wearing the queenly crown—had been mere window dressing. Any good-looking girl would have been just as fine. But now came the moment God had been setting up for; *now* was the time when having His chosen person in place was about to pay off.

Let me repeat our earlier theme: If you're a common, ungifted person—an Eleanor Rigby, a Don Knotts—then God needs you. For some specific purpose, He needs you. You may have a small, unnoticed, unheralded talent or ability, but He needs it. And He needs it now, at this very moment. No one in the body of Christ is unnecessary; the apostle Paul's letter is beautifully clear on that point.

And yet, it's so often the case, back in Bible times and today, that something big also lies ahead. You may have an Esther experience in front of you. Your quiet, seemingly insignificant life may someday be in the limelight of history.

And here's my question: Are you preparing *now* for that moment?

Consider the Bible story of Joseph. We kind of like that story here at the *Voice of Prophecy*. That young man went through two stretches of time where it looked as though God had forgotten him! His talents were going to be wasted; with all his natural abilities and spiritual gifts, he wasn't doing much more than pushing a broom for Potiphar and then later for the jailer of the Egyptian Penitentiary.

But it's very interesting how Joseph reacted. He didn't give up! He didn't say, "Well, now I'm nobody; I'm dispensable. I guess I'll quit." He did two things. First of all, he kept serving in the ways he could. Even with diminished opportunities, he kept on using the gifts he could use. If all he could do was sweep, fine; he'd sweep.

However, he did something else. He kept in readiness for a future big moment, just in case it might come. He kept growing in grace, growing in ability, growing in influence. He added to his list of friends. He did favors where he could—not just hoping for a payback later, but because that's the way things are done in God's kingdom.

And finally, when God moved all the puzzle pieces around on the table and orchestrated events so that he had that prime minister's spot all opened up, Joseph was ready to move in. Tanned, rested, and ready to serve, as we say. His faithfulness during the quiet, no-headline years finally paid off.

We can also look at the life of our Saviour, Jesus Christ. What did He do from the time He was born until His ministry really began at the age of thirty? We don't know! The Bible gives very little indication. We have that one story where He was lost, and Mom and Dad found Him teaching in the temple. We have that favorite memory verse over in Luke 2:52: "And Jesus grew in wisdom and stature, and in favor with God and man."

And we do have the verse right before that one, where the Bible tells us that Jesus went to Nazareth with His parents and was obedient to them. But that's about all we know. We know that the Boy Jesus, and then the Teenager Jesus, and then the Man Jesus spent *thirty* years getting ready for *three*. Thirty quiet, unmentioned years preparing for the three most pivotal years in the history of the universe.

And I suppose that makes us think for a moment about a girl named Mary, the mother of Jesus. What do we know about her? Practically nothing! What kind of a child was she? How was she raised? How did she get ready to be the mother of the Saviour of mankind? We don't know the answers to those questions.

But here was one very quiet life; before the Holy Spirit moved upon her, she wasn't well-known. Her name and face weren't on the evening news every evening. But somehow, some way, she had made herself ready. And Heaven chose her. An angel of the Lord came down and told her she had found favor with God. Her aunt Elizabeth, speaking prophetically, said to this young girl: "Blessed are you among women, and blessed is the fruit of your womb" (Luke 1:42, NRSV).

Yes, we often lose sight of the quiet years, don't we, where someone gets ready. But that's such an important part of being in the body of Christ.

Often in a human body, certain parts aren't used—or aren't used much—until a moment of great importance arrives. There's a burning building, and a child is stuck up on the fifth floor. All at once that dad or mom is able to do herculean things, and muscles that hadn't really done much up until then suddenly give power to that miraculous accomplishment. There's a deadly infection or a life-threatening cut, and the body digs deep and rushes white blood cells to the scene or employs its coagulating properties to heal itself.

But it's the body that was kept in basic readiness that's able to rise to the heroic moment, isn't it?

Back in 1988—returning to baseball now—the Dodgers traded to get a power hitter named Mike Davis from the Oakland A's. And he just messed up terribly. He couldn't hit at all! Major disappointment! After a couple of months, the Dodgers plopped him down on the bench, and he simply disappeared from view. Kirk Gibson and Mike Marshall were hitting a lot of home runs, and they just didn't need Mike Davis. His talents weren't required. Game after game, month after month, he didn't play a single minute.

But do you know something? He kept himself ready. He sat on the bench and encouraged others. He kept in shape. He took batting practice every day. He still thought of himself as a home-run hitter who, right now, wasn't getting the chance to hit home runs. He did what he could and he stayed in readiness.

Well, it got to be the World Series. Dodgers against those same Oakland A's. All at once, Kirk Gibson was out with an injury. Maybe you remember that. Mike Marshall was out.

Brought to L.A. for One At-bat

Just about everyone was out; half the lineup was in the hospital instead of in the dugout. David and I were kind of hoping *we* might get a call from Tommy Lasorda; after all, we've played a little ball. But in game 5 of the World Series, that frantic manager finally had to turn to Mike Davis because he had nowhere else to turn. "You're in, Mike," he said.

It came down to the late innings. Dodgers up by a run, and up three games to one, but everyone in America knew that the bats of Oakland's mighty Jose Canseco and Mark McGuire might wake up at any moment and start bashing homers again. Anything could happen.

Bench-riding Mike Davis, who had been quietly waiting and preparing for months, came up to bat with a man on base. The count went three balls and no strikes. For some reason, manager Tommy Lasorda gave this substitute player, this *nothing* performer, the green light. "Swing away if you like the pitch."

Mike Davis swung 3-0 . . . and hit a monster home run to put the game and the 1988 World Series on ice. He got the one swing of the bat he'd been brought here to get. He was ready to get his one moment.

Tell me, friend. Are you taking your batting practice each day? Just in case?

CHAPTER 14

"Lean on Me"

Eric Liddell, Olympic runner from Scotland, would not run on Sunday in the 1924 Olympic Games in Paris. That's the one-line description of the beautiful and inspiring cinematic achievement Christians know as *Chariots of Fire*. Liddell, in order to qualify for the 100-meter race, would have to qualify in a heat run on Sunday. He wouldn't do it. "Runner Puts God Before King!" screamed the newspaper headlines.

Well, you know that Eric Liddell ran instead in the 400-meter competition, a much more difficult race—not his specialty. And won the gold medal there as he "ran for God."

Earlier in the film, perhaps you recall a scene where a little boy is kicking a football around on Sunday morning as Eric and his family come out of church. Very kindly, very graciously, Eric says to the boy, "You know, the Sabbath isn't a day for football. I'll meet you here tomorrow, and we'll have a game then." And we see a consistent message coming from this very dedicated Christian athlete.

At the end of the story is a brief announcement, telling us that Eric Liddell did fulfill his lifelong ambition of being a missionary to China. And that when he died in a Japanese prisoner-of-war camp, "all of Scotland mourned."

But perhaps you never heard one tiny postscript to the story. Eric Liddell, faithful, dedicated Sunday keeper, found himself in that POW camp. And because of his spiritual stature, his integrity—and maybe because he was an Olympic hero—people looked up to him in that camp. He became one of the strong pillars that others leaned on. The weak, the discouraged, the despondent . . . they came to depend on Eric Liddell.

There was also a small group of boys locked up in that camp. Frustrated and cooped up and hungry and feisty, they began to argue and to kick and flail away at each other as boys will. They'd try to play a game of soccer there in the prison yard, but the games would inevitably end up in an argument and a fistfight.

And then one day Eric Liddell, the missionary hero so many depended on, the quiet man who was the tower of strength to all the others, came over to where the boys were. He helped organize them into teams. He refereed the game. He showed them how to play clean and fair and how to be good opponents. He made sure tempers stayed calm and that Jesus was the center focus of even their playtime together.

What day of the week was it? Friend, it was Sunday morning.

Eric Liddell wouldn't do his own pleasure on what he believed to be his Sabbath. He wouldn't seek his own glory. But he was willing to join those little boys in kicking a soccer ball, if that's what it took to be their tower of strength.

I don't tell you that story in order to start a debate about proper Sabbath observance. But I find in this simple World War II story a plain Bible truth, and that's this: God needs His strong men, His strong women, in the body of Christ. In every body there are strong parts and weaker parts. And what a blessing it is when the strong parts live up to their ordained function.

In 1 Corinthians 12:21, Paul directs his words to those in the church who might be tempted to feel that they're more important than the others. "The eye cannot say to the hand, 'I don't need you!' And the head cannot say to the feet, 'I don't need you!' "

We could make a quick and effective point out of this very object lesson. Yes, the eye can look at things and take in visual impressions—without the help of the hand. But what a stilted life, a frustrating existence . . . if you saw flowers, but couldn't ever use your hand to pick them. If you saw the lovely face of your wife, but couldn't reach out to caress her cheek. As important and necessary and maybe even exalted a "body position" as the eyes hold, they need the hands if they're to be fulfilled, don't they? And we could make a similar point about the head and the feet. The feet take the body where the head decides it would be good to go.

But let's take it a step further. Not only are the strong parts not to dismiss the weaker or less glamorous parts—I believe the body of Christ is called upon to have strong parts lift and carry weak ones! Strong, faithful champions are needed in the church of Christ, for those who are weaker to lean on.

In his book, *The Victorious Christian Life*, Pastor Tony Evans says this about strong believers: "As members of the Body of Christ, we are like the pieces of a jigsaw puzzle. Each piece has *protrusions* and *indentations*. The protrusions represent our strengths (gifts, talents, abilities) and the indentations represent our weaknesses (faults, shortcomings, undeveloped areas). The beautiful thing is that when we assemble, each piece complements the other, blending inconspicuously to produce a beautiful picture."

You know, Jesus had something to say to one of His strong disciples—at least Peter thought he was strong. On a Thursday evening right before Gethsemane and Calvary, just hours before Jesus' own crucifixion, His great concern was for His twelve weak disciples. He wanted to strengthen and encourage them; He wanted to warn them and protect them. But He knew that in just a few hours He was going to be taken away and nailed to a tree. And He turned and said to Peter: "Simon, Simon, Satan has asked to sift you as wheat. But I have prayed for you, Simon, that your faith may not fail." Now notice this. "And when you have turned back, *strengthen your brothers*" (Luke 22:31, 32).

Aren't those three words powerful? If you're strong, Jesus says, strengthen your brothers. And your sisters! Be a pillar to those who need a pillar. Be a rock others can lean against.

Maybe you're thinking to yourself, "Pastor Lonnie, you don't know me. I'm one of the weak ones! I'm a baby in the faith! I'm the one who does the leaning in our church!" And that may well be true.

But isn't it also possible that there is someone out there even weaker? Someone who needs, in a way that perhaps you've never thought of, *your* kind of strength? You may be very weak and stumbling in many areas, but I believe there's something in your experience, some area, some slice of spiritual life where *you* have strength to offer.

Think about this. Jesus, the strongest, bravest, most courageous Christian who ever lived, needed someone that Thursday evening in Gethsemane. He begged His disciples to stay with Him and pray with Him and comfort Him. What a heartbreaking tragedy that angels from heaven had to come down and give the strength and share the comfort that Peter and James and John failed to provide!

Let me share a story with you that comes directly out of one of our recent radio series, *The Care and Feeding of Pastors*.

Edith was a dress designer in New York City. She was comfortable moving in the world of culture and manners. She was meticulous and exact in everything she did.

Her new pastor, on the other hand, was exasperatingly absent-minded. Older members in the church would do things for him, and he would never even say Thank you. People would get sick, and he would fail to show up at the hospital. And then Edith would hear about it.

Probably the worst thing of all—this fellow wore *terrible* ties. They were absolutely dreadful, almost an abomination.

What was Edith to do?

What she did was call him. The older members who confided in Edith their discontent or their hurt never knew. No one else in the church ever knew. But every time Edith learned of some social gaffe by her pastor, she would as graciously as possible let him know. She told him she knew he had meant no offense, and she was a little bit embarrassed to tell him, but she thought he would want to know so he could make things right. She never attacked him; she just informed him when there was some way he could smooth ruffled feathers or earn his way back into the good graces of some of the old-timers in the church.

But let me add this. Edith didn't just speak to her pastor about his mistakes. She also enabled him to make maximum use of his strengths. In spite of his absentmindedness, she saw in him a wisdom and spiritual maturity out of proportion to his years. In conversations, he had a surprising tact. She frequently invited non-Christian friends and neighbors for dinner and an evening of conversation, and included her pastor in the group because she could count on him to speak about God and faith in a way that would touch even thick-skinned New Yorkers.

Best of all, she took care of his awful ties with a Christmas present.

Despite this pastor's mistakes and weaknesses, the church experienced dramatic growth, quadrupling its attendance in five years and drawing large numbers of young people. If you asked the pastor today the reason for the growth of his church, one of the first factors he would mention, after the grace of God, would be Edith.

Right now, look into your spiritual mirror. Ask God to show you where you can be a strength to someone. Is there a letter you could write? Could you encourage someone a bit more often? Be a more appealing example to that easily tempted co-worker? Maybe even buy a new tie for your pastor and give it to him this Christmas!

God needs His champions. Every age needs an Eric Liddell. Or maybe an Erica Liddell. Every church needs one, every office, every home. If you're reading this chapter, I think you're probably the very one God has in mind.

CHAPTER 15

Hostage Terry Anderson's New Church

Every now and then, a letter comes to us here at Box 55, Los Angeles, and it basically says this: "Pastor Lonnie, I really consider you and the *Voice of Prophecy* to be MY church. I went to church here in town for years but, you know, the pastor had some problems, and people were critical, and the treasurer didn't handle our funds right. So about two years ago, I quit going . . . but I listen to you every single weekend. I'm enclosing a contribution—this is basically my church offering—and I want to thank you for being my church."

How do you respond to a letter like that? On the one hand, we're truly sorry for the circumstances this person finds himself in. And frankly, it's kind of hard not to be grateful for gifts that come in; after all, we depend on financial contributions. But speaking very honestly, none of us at the *Voice of Prophecy* want to serve in the place of a person's local church. And right here I'd like to explore with you the clear Bible reasons why we very humbly want to turn down that role.

A few years ago, in the December 16, 1991, issue of *Newsweek* was a fascinating story about newly released hostage Terry Anderson. For 2,455 days, Terry had been held in captivity in Beirut, Lebanon. That's nearly seven years being held in tiny, dark, damp cells. Seven years of psychological warfare; later he told how once the guards gave him a new suit of clothes because he was about to be released. He wore it for a week—and then the guards came and told him to get undressed and give the suit back because, "Stupid fool, you aren't going *anywhere*."

When he finally got out, the thing that amazed journalists was how psychologically strong this Associated Press bureau chief seemed to be. After seven years of undergoing unbelievable strain, Terry Anderson appeared to be cheerful, strong, even good-humored. In fact, the title to the four-page magazine article was this: "How Terry Survived."

From the very beginning of the 2,455 days, Anderson became a kind of squad leader. He insisted that the hostages all keep their cell clean. He made a deck of cards out of little bits of paper and a chess set out of pieces of tin foil. The men taught each other French and Arabic. When the guards finally gave him a Bible, he memorized huge sections out of it.

But there's one more thing these men did. Terry Anderson and the other hostages went to church. They formed their own church body and had regular services. Some were Catholics, others Protestants—but together they formed what they called, tongue-in-cheek, "The Church of the Locked Door." Terry, who went back to his early Catholic roots, knotted himself a rosary from string plucked out of the plastic floor mats in their prison. And *Newsweek* said this about the secret of this church's spiritual success: "He

[Anderson] built on the hostages' greatest strength—*each other*."

Week after week, when one prisoner was struggling, there was another to encourage him. When one was tempted to give up, someone else would remind him that they had vowed to stick together and survive. When one of the men was tempted to hate their captors—and you could certainly understand the almost overpowering desire to fall into that trap—another man would be right there to share the gospel message of forgiveness and the example of Jesus under similar circumstances. These men needed the church, even if it was "The Church of the Locked Door."

Now back to those occasional letters we get from listeners. I know full well there are people who are shut-ins. They're too sick to get to church. We have prisoners who listen, and they're not free to walk down the street to the nearest Christian church. We have people living in isolation, a hundred miles away from the nearest organized body of believers. So, yes, there are people for whom the *Voice of Prophecy* is their church. They don't have any choice, and we're glad to be on the radio to serve their spiritual needs.

But if you live where you *could* go to church, if you've left the fellowship of believers for other reasons . . . then I believe the Bible has some straight and sobering truth for you to consider today. Friend, God's Word *commands* His people to be in church! Let me share with you another very challenging statement from *The Body*, by former Watergate conspirator Chuck Colson and Ellen Santilli Vaughn.

"It is scandalous that so many believers today have such a low view of the church. They see their Christian lives as a solitary exercise—Jesus and me—or they treat the church as a building or a social center. They flit from congregation to congregation—or they don't associate with any church at all. That the church is held in such low esteem reflects not only the depths of our biblical ignorance, but the alarming extent to which we have succumbed to the obsessive individualism of modern culture."

Now here's a followup thought from that same book: "Of course every believer is part of the *universal* church. But for any Christian who has a choice in the matter, failure to cleave to a particular church is failure to obey Christ" (emphasis supplied).

Perhaps you're saying to yourself, "Well, OK, that's Colson's opinion." Take a look at the book of Ephesians where Paul talks about this very same question. In fact, chapter 4, in our New International Version, is subtitled "Unity in the Body of Christ." Here's verses 12-16, describing the purpose of the church:

"To prepare God's people for works of service, so that the body of Christ may be built up until we all reach unity in the faith and in the knowledge of the Son of God and become mature, attaining to the whole measure of the fullness of Christ. Then we will no longer be infants, tossed back and forth by the waves, and blown here and there by every wind of teaching and by the cunning and craftiness of men in their deceitful scheming. Instead, speaking the truth in love, we will in all things grow up into Him who is the Head, that is, Christ."

Notice this final verse: "From Him the whole body, *joined and held together* by every supporting ligament, grows and builds itself up in love, as each part does its work."

No wonder the writer of Hebrews spoke in such direct terms about the idea of staying at home by the fireplace and just listening to Christian radio. Notice these words in chapter 10: "Let us consider how we may spur one another on toward love and good deeds. *Let us not give up meeting together*, as some are in the habit of doing, but let us encourage one another—and all the more as you see the Day approaching" (10:24, 25).

Perhaps you've heard it put this way from the King James:

"Not forsaking the assembling of ourselves together."

Dr. Tony Evans explores the Ephesians passage and then makes this comment: "Our relationship to the corporate body of Christians is crucial to the progress of the growth of our personal relationship with God."

Just two pages later, Tony adds this keen observation: "No, you don't have to go to church to be saved. Yes, you can worship God in your heart. But you do need the church to keep you on track. You do need the church to keep you accountable. You do need the church to care for you during the disasters of your life. You do need the church to encourage you as you keep walking down the right way. You don't need the church to be saved but you need it to make sure you're living like you're saved."

I can't help but think about Pastor H. M. S. Richards, who for so many years and decades spoke from our VOP microphone. He had people who considered him to be their pastor, and the *Voice of Prophecy* was their church. And many, many times he would encourage his audience to actually move away from their radios and get in their cars and go to their own church.

Maybe their pastor had some struggles. Pastor Richards was acquainted with a lot of faithful pastors who weren't quite perfect yet; he knew about that. Maybe that local church had its internal divisions and its arguing factions. Over the years Harold and Ken and their dad visited hundreds of Christian churches where he was a guest speaker, and they saw all of that. But still, he always believed that the local Christian church, faulty and frail as it might be, was the place where God's people should go—not now and then, but fifty-two weeks a year.

The gifts that many of you send to the *Voice of Prophecy*—and we surely appreciate them—should never be sent until you've fulfilled your financial obligations to your own local Christian church. When you've given what God has impressed you to give to that body of believers, if you have additional funds you choose to invest in this radio ministry, wonderful! We praise God for that gift and for that spirit and for *you*! But the needs of your own church come ahead of the *Voice of Prophecy* or any other adjunct ministry you might currently be supporting. That's a biblical principle we want to fully support.

Well, this section in our book is coming to a close. This weekend your brothers and sisters are gathering together. Some of them are strong, and some of them are weak. They have things to share that you need—and God's given you gifts to share that they need. You may be a home-run hitter for the team; you may be one who sits on the bench. You're just there so the Mike Piazzas and the Hakeem Alajuwons and Steve Youngs have someone to sit next to when *they're* on the bench. But friend, you're part of the team. The team's not all there unless you're there. The body isn't complete unless you take your place with them.

We'll see you with the team, in church, this weekend.

7—P.P.G.

SECTION 4

A Bride Makes Herself Ready

CHAPTER 16

Countdown to the Wedding March

T-minus ninety minutes. Everything was ready for the countdown. The decorations in the church were all in place: every ribbon, every flower, every candle, even the long white-ribboned trail down the center aisle. The musicians had their music ready; the groomsmen were already dressed in their tuxedos. Even the preacher had already arrived at the church and was ready to pose for pictures with the happy couple.

But one thing still wasn't ready.

The bride.

For two days she'd been working on her hair, and one little spot just wouldn't go into place. The hairdresser kept working on her and applying can after can of hairspray, but the total picture was one of just-slightly-less-than-perfection. It wasn't quite "there."

When she finally got to the point where the hair was all

right, they went to the face and the makeup. Well, that wasn't exactly right either. The eyeliner didn't quite work; somehow it clashed with the hair color. But when the bride and the maid of honor tried a darker shade, it made her look kind of vampy and cheap—and they didn't want that.

By now it was "T-minus twenty-five minutes." And when the bride stood up, she saw that her dress had a couple of wrinkles in it. There wasn't time to take it off and work on it, so she and a couple of girls began to try to steam out the wrinkles while she still had it on. Then they all noticed that a couple of the buttons were a little off-center. Why hadn't they seen that before? And now the veil didn't hang quite right; it looked droopy.

"T-minus ten minutes." The photographer poked his head in the door. "Aren't we taking any pictures at all before the ceremony?" he wanted to know. The bride could feel beads of perspiration pop out on her forehead . . . and, of course, that began to ruin her makeup. She looked in the mirror and saw that the one hair-sprayed curl had popped loose again and was now sticking straight up in the back like Alfalfa's in The Little Rascals. She twisted around to try to reach for the hair-spray can, and felt a ripping sound.

T-minus two minutes . . . T-minus one minute . . . and "Here Comes the Bride."

With all due apologies for the agonizing memories I'm sure this introduction brings back, we want to open our Bibles now and talk about the topic of Christian perfection. And probably those last ninety minutes before a wedding reveal one of the most meaningful quests for perfection that any of us can recall.

God's Word calls the Christian church "the bride of Christ." You and I, as believers, are part of that metaphor. God also commands us to be perfect. You can read that in Matthew 5:48, right in the Sermon on the Mount: "Be perfect, therefore, as your heavenly Father is perfect."

It's interesting, and maybe comforting, to notice that it doesn't say, "Be *as* perfect as your heavenly Father is." And we'll explore that distinction. But it does say, "*Be* perfect, as He is perfect."

If you read back through chapter 5 to discover the context, which is always a good idea, you find that Christ has been talking about loving your enemies. Loving those who persecute you. Then comes this challenge to be perfect.

Back to our bride struggling with the hairspray and the ironing board in the dressing room of the church. She has a desire to become perfect in the next ninety minutes. When she walks down the aisle to meet her beloved, it's her heart's desire that she be a picture of radiant perfection. She wants the groom to look at her and see nothing but perfection—not a spot or a wrinkle.

And how come? I find that as I keep the motif of a bride and a groom and a wedding day in my thinking while studying this Bible subject, it provides me with a healthy perspective. What is the purpose of character perfection? Why would we strive for it? Why *should* we strive for it? What does it prove or accomplish? Is the bridegroom looking for it . . . and what will He say or do if we don't measure up?

What does it mean in the Bible when it says, "Be perfect"? How can we define this very open-ended, horizon-expanding word?

It's very clear that, whatever the Bible means, "perfect" is a word describing something real, something that *can* be accomplished. In Job 1:1, this man named Job was perfect, the Bible tells us. "That man was perfect and upright, and one that feared God, and eschewed evil" (KJV).

The NIV softens these words of praise; it calls Job "blameless and upright," a man who feared God and shunned evil. But whatever the Bible is thinking of when it says "perfect," Job was doing it.

In the book of Leviticus, those who brought lambs to be

offered as sacrifices were to bring perfect lambs. So there was such a thing as perfection in that area.

One of the Old Testament kings named Asa is described as having a heart that was "perfect with the Lord all his days." In the NIV: a heart "fully committed to the Lord" (1 Kings 15:14). This in describing a man who loved God and tore down all the idols in Judah—but didn't even fully succeed in that. And yet he had what God called a perfect heart.

We printed out the dictionary's many definitions of the word "perfect" so as to have a workable *secular* platform on which to stand. Notice a few of these.

1. Lacking nothing essential to the whole; complete of its nature or kind.

2. Being without defect or blemish: a perfect specimen. (Can you see how that sacrificial lamb would qualify?)

3. Thoroughly skilled or talented in a certain field or area; proficient.

4. Completely suited for a particular purpose or situation: "She was the perfect actress for the part."

5. Completely corresponding to a description, standard, or type: "a perfect circle, a perfect gentleman."

6. Complete, thorough, utter: "a perfect fool." (That's an interesting illustration—and hopefully, a definition you and I *don't* fit!)

7. Pure; undiluted; unmixed: "perfect red."

8. Excellent and delightful in all respects: "a perfect day."

And it goes on from there. So we ask again: Can a bride be perfect? Can a *Christian* be perfect?

I think back to a bride who came slowly and majestically to the altar in the year 1967. Her name was Jeannie Jones—and that day she became Jeannie Jones Melashenko. And I should have persuaded the staff at Pacific Press to drop in a twelve-page photo insert of our wedding pictures and you could see for yourself what a *perfect* bride looks like.

Now, did Jeannie Jones bring perfection to that wedding altar on August 27, 1967? Was she absolutely without defect or blemish? No, probably not. Underneath that beautiful, nearly perfect hairdo and wedding dress were probably a couple of bumps and cavities and scars and tissue cells that eventually will grow old and give way. We all have them; we all bring a bit of frailty to the wedding feast.

Did she "*completely* correspond to the standard, the benchmark"? Did she set the bridal standard for all time, with absolutely no room for improvement? Again, probably not . . . and I trust she'll still let me into the house and let me have supper with her.

But let me pose this one: Was she "excellent and delightful in all respects?" Did she bring a "pure and undiluted" loyalty into our marriage? Was she completely suited to the purpose of being my loyal Christian partner in life? Did she express a complete and utter and thorough devotion to our exclusive relationship, our love for each other?

Of course she did! My wife Jeannie was *and is* a "perfect" wife! In the respects that count, she has been my perfect bride for more than twenty-eight years.

I believe God looks for perfection in His bride with the eyes of a groom. He's not looking for a list—He's looking for a loyalty. He's not seeking a dandruff-free hairdo—He's seeking a completely dedicated heart.

Let me say this as well: we're going to study perfection . . . but not perfectionISM. Perfectionism is the belief that our perfection, no matter how it's defined, is in any way a part of what qualifies us for God's kingdom. PerfectionISM makes our performance, our achieving, our successes in the bridal dressing room—the criterion of salvation. Every bride, and every Christian who is part of being the bride of Christ, must reject the deadly heresy of perfectionism.

Can we be the kind of perfection the Groom is looking for? Yes, we can. Turn the page and let's find out more.

CHAPTER 17

Trying to Get to Sleep

Last summer, I returned home from spending two weeks in the city of Utrecht in the Netherlands. I was there for the quinquennial world congress, or General Conference, of my Seventh-day Adventist Church family, and serving as the TV anchor for the satellite TV broadcasting that they beamed back to the U.S. and Canada during the ten-day event.

All very exciting and thrilling . . . but that's not the topic of the moment. What I want to reminisce about is my hotel room in the little neighboring town of Bunnik.

For some reason, we hit Holland during the heat wave of the summer. It was in the very high eighties and nineties almost every single day we were there. And humid—wet and sticky.

Two factors really added to the ambience. First, no air conditioning in the hotel. Which, considering the usual temperatures in that country, I could probably forgive. But secondly, in the middle of the summer, the sun goes down about ten-thirty in the evening. So all afternoon and into the late night, sunshine was just beating down on the side of that hotel, melting everyone staying there.

This all combined to make it very, very difficult to sleep. You'd lie there at night, without any covers over you, feeling those beads of sweat start to form. And all you could think about was, "It's one in the morning and I'm still awake. Now it's one-thirty. Still awake. Two o'clock, no sleep. I've got to get to sleep. Why can't I sleep? How am I going to feel tomorrow if I don't get some sleep soon? *Three* o'clock, still no sleep." On and on it went.

And do you see the dilemma? As long as I was focusing on my need for sleep and thinking about sleep and how I wasn't getting any sleep . . . what happened? Well, you've been through it too. Sleep is the hardest thing in the world to achieve if that's what you're aiming your emotional energy at.

This has quite a bit to do with our biblical topic of perfection. What does it mean to *be* perfect? What did Jesus mean when He challenged us to be perfect?

The Bible has references that talk very plainly about perfection. Many other passages imply it. I read in Matthew, chapter 28, where Christ tells His followers: "Go and make disciples of all nations, baptizing them in the name of the Father and of the Son and of the Holy Spirit, and teaching them to *obey EVERYTHING* I have commanded you."

Is it possible to obey everything? Is it possible and necessary to *perfectly* obey? In Revelation 14, the faithful saints of the last days are described: "These are they which follow the Lamb whithersoever He goeth. These were redeemed from among men, being the firstfruits unto God and to the Lamb." Now what comes next? "And in their mouth was found *no guile*: for they are *without fault* before the throne of God."

These people follow perfectly; they obey perfectly. In the last chapter, we discovered that the Scriptures define perfection as an attainable goal. Genesis 6:9 says that Noah was "a just man and perfect in his generations" (KJV.) "Blameless," another version says, "a man who walked with God." Considering Noah, who later got drunk and forgot to get dressed one morning, as *perfect* may mold or adjust your picture of the concept of perfection a bit, but let's continue.

But would you join me in addressing this question? What should our *focus* be as Christians? Do we *try* to be perfect? Do we strive for perfection?

My pastor friend Morris Venden has for many years been a popular speaker at religious retreats and camp meetings. Now, I think you'll understand when I observe that when you go to "camp meetings" and religious services in the big tent somewhere where 2,000 attendees are gathered, you meet people of all persuasions and backgrounds. When it comes to religious theories and ideas, you're likely to encounter just about anything.

After Venden preached one evening—and the subject of sinless perfection had come up—a man came up to him and said, with a certain proud gleam in his eyes, "I haven't sinned for two years!"

There was kind of a pause. After all, what do you say to a claim like that one? Finally Venden responded, "Is that right?"

"Yes," the man went on. He described how he'd gained the victory over *every* sin, every temptation. There wasn't any excuse for sinning, he said. The Bible commands us to be perfect, and that's exactly what he'd done. Temptation had no power over him anymore, and he was heading into his third year of sinless perfection.

Well, as I mentioned in the last chapter, this man wasn't really focusing on perfection as much as he was on perfectionISM. Man, his two years of error-free living better count for something! They were like college credits! He wanted to be sure that Venden and the whole camp meeting population were aware of his achievement.

About a year later, as Venden tells the story, he was at a camp meeting, and guess who should walk up? The same man stood before him and stuck his chin out a little bit. "Remember me?" he asked.

Venden looked straight back at him. "How could I forget?" he responded.

And, you know, maybe we're more like that man than we're willing to admit. How often have you caught yourself thinking about your progress, wanting some credit for it? "How am I doing? Am I almost there yet? Am I obeying? Am I obeying perfectly?" It's almost like that frantic late-night mental buzz that keeps you from getting any sleep.

In one of his books entitled "Beyond Personality," which is the third part of C. S. Lewis' *Mere Christianity*, the author addresses this twin-towers question of perfection and our human focus. In the chapter, "Is Christianity Easy or Hard," he says: "When Christ said, 'Be perfect,' He meant it. He meant that we must go in for the whole treatment."

Then in the next chapter, entitled "Counting the Cost," he amplifies it, explaining that many people were unhappy with him over what he meant.

"Some people seem to think," he writes, "that this means, 'Unless you are perfect, I [Christ] will not help you'; and as we cannot be perfect, then, if He meant that, our position is hopeless. But I do not think He did mean that. I think He meant 'The only help I will give is help to become perfect. You may want something less: but I will give you nothing less.' "

You know, that kind of shifts the whole battle scene; it's a brand new paradigm, as people are fond of saying now. "Be ye perfect," Christ says, and then He makes Himself responsible for getting us to that state . . . *whatever it is*. On the very next page, Lewis adds another insight:

"That is why He warned people to 'count the cost' before becoming Christians. 'Make no mistake,' He says, 'if you let Me, I will make you perfect. The moment you put yourself in My hands, that is what you are in for. Nothing less, or other, than that. You have free will, and if you choose, you can push Me away. But if you do not push Me away, understand that I am going to see this job through. I will never rest, nor let you rest, until you are literally perfect—until My Father can say without reservation that He is well pleased with you, as He said He was well pleased with Me. THIS I CAN DO AND WILL DO. But I will not do anything less.' "

Friend, do you see then why we sing, "I Surrender All"? And in singing that, the responsibility for perfection, as defined in God's terms, becomes His? It becomes His goal for you; it becomes something He accomplishes in your life, in His way and according to His timetable.

What, then, should be our focus? On perfection itself . . . or on getting to know the God who will give perfection? Do we think about the ladder or the Saviour who is holding the ladder? As Venden writes in another of his books, "Don't dwell on perfection, dwell on Jesus."

And I will say this. Those who are focusing on Jesus and getting to know and trust Him more . . . they're *not* going to be the ones noticing or commenting on their own sinlessness. At camp meeting or at any other place. One of my favorite writers, E. G. White, had this to say in her classic Christian bestseller, *Christ's Object Lessons*: "The nearer we come to Jesus and the more clearly we discern the purity of His character, the more clearly we shall discern the exceeding sinfulness of sin and the less we shall feel like exalting ourselves."

It's safe to say that those who reach heaven's definition of perfection will be the last to know or to boast. They'll be singing about Jesus, not about their own victories.

Trying to Get to Sleep

I like the way Marvin Moore writes about perfection in his book, *The Crisis of the End Time*. He suggests that even the Bible definition of "perfection" isn't something we can fully grasp or define. Which dictionary definition do we pick? He doesn't know, and he suggests that we can't know, either. But then he says this: "We don't know what perfection is or how to get there, but when we do our part, God is responsible for getting us there."

You know, I like that. And I like how he links that truth to the Bible story where God said to Abraham: "I want you to go to a country that I'll show you."

"Sure," Abraham said. "Where is it?"

And God answered: "I'm not going to tell you. Just get started, and I'll make Myself responsible to get you there."

What did Abraham do? He started walking . . . and God guided him.

That's much the same as our quest, isn't it? Where are we going? That's God's responsibility. How shall we get there? That's His responsibility too. But we *can* start walking.

CHAPTER 18

Can God Save the Queen?

Recently Jeannie and I were in England helping some of our Christian brothers and sisters there celebrate fifty years of *Voice of Prophecy* broadcasting in their country. What a marvelous experience to meet so many people for whom this radio program has had a meaningful part!

But being so recently in London brings to mind an illustration that sheds a bright light on our topic of Christian perfection. I'm borrowing this illustration from a friend and writer, Pastor Roy Adams, who is one of the editors of the official church paper for my denomination. In his recent book entitled *The Nature of Christ*, Adams writes about the current monarch of England, Queen Elizabeth.

According to recent financial reports, he says, the queen is worth something like eight billion dollars. She's right up there close to Bill Gates, who they say is the world's richest person right now. Certainly she's number

1 in the British Empire.

Now here's the question Adams poses. Is Queen Elizabeth a sinner? Has she attained perfection, or is she a common sinner? He asks the question and talks openly about her financial status because she's admittedly a very public figure. Let me quote his direct observation:

"In my estimation, the queen of England is one of the most decent people in the world. You won't find her engaged in gossip or brawls; you won't find her in nightclubs or pubs. As for carousing and wild parties, don't even mention them. Foul language never crosses her lips, and she is abusive to no one. The epitome of purity and high morals, she commands the respect of the whole world, notwithstanding the foibles and failings of members of the royal family in recent years."

But then Adams goes on. Notice: "But . . . with millions starving to death today, think of the queen approaching Jesus (with $8 billion stashed away in various banks and securities) and asking Him: 'Good Master, what must I do to have eternal life?' What do you think Jesus would say to Her Majesty?"

It's an interesting question, isn't it? If sin is simply "doing bad things" and if perfection is simply avoiding bad behavior, then we'd have to agree that Queen Elizabeth has reached Christian perfection. In fact, we'd have to go back to that man at that religious camp meeting who claimed that he hadn't sinned in the past two years—and give him credit for two years of "perfection."

But what if sin—and perfection—are much more? What if all the things you *fail* to do are also sin? What if every kind word you could have said, but didn't, is sin? What if every generous deed you could have performed, but didn't, is a sin? What if missing the mark is a sin? From that perspective, the queen of England is still a long way off, and you and I are perhaps many miles from the target.

Adams shares a cute story about a boy who was asked what "sins of omission" might be. The kid thought for a moment and then said: "Sins of omission are sins I should have committed, but didn't!"

Well, speaking of "missing the mark," that faulty definition certainly qualifies, doesn't it? But right now I'd like to go hand-in-hand with you into one of the more thought-provoking areas of Christian Bible study. And let me give credit again to Pastor Roy Adams, and this wonderful book, *The Nature of Christ*, which includes a chapter entitled "What Is Sin?" Of course, we can't adequately describe perfection until we know what the Bible considers sin to be.

I John 3:4 contains the classic short definition of sin: "Sin is the trangression of the law."

As Christians, we accept that. But are there deeper meanings to these words? Adams takes us to Psalm 32, one of King David's well-known penitential prayers. And in just two verses, we discover here four painful, and yet very educational, descriptions of what sin is.

"Blessed is he whose *transgression* is forgiven, whose *sin* is covered. Blessed is the man unto whom the Lord imputeth not *iniquity*, and in whose spirit there is no *guile*."

Transgression, sin, iniquity, and guile. But do all four of these words mean the same thing? Is it just sin-sin-sin-and sin . . . or is there more here?

Verse 1: "Blessed is he whose *transgression* is forgiven."

Transgression comes from the Hebrew word *pesha*, signifying "rebellion," a "departure from God." It implies willful, deliberate sin, rebellious sin, a shaking of the fist, so to speak.

Let's go to the second definition, from the expression: "Blessed is he . . . whose *sin* is covered."

The word *sin* in this phrase comes from the Hebrew *chatta'ah*, which refers to sin from the point of view of missing the mark, failing to do one's duty. That's according to two excellent Bible commentaries that Adams refers to. We get here the picture of a queen of England not giving away all she could, a man or woman not doing all the good deeds they might have done. Their hearts may be right, but they fall short.

Now let's examine the third distinct interpretation. "Blessed is the man unto whom the Lord imputeth not *iniquity*."

What does this mean—*iniquity*? In Hebrew, that comes from the word *awon*, which refers to "moral distortion" or "crookedness" or just plain "guilt." Roy Adams quotes from the *Interpreter's Dictionary of the Bible*, which describes this as an inner state that is deformed, perverse, twisted. This is a kind of sinfulness that's part of our inner being, our innate sinful nature.

Now number 4: "And in whose spirit there is no *guile*."

Now that's a word we have some inkling about. *Guile* makes us think of sneakiness, of slippery deception. Sure enough, the Hebrew word here, *remiyyah*, means exactly that: deceit, falsehood, duplicity. We're reminded of our own private Watergates and Whitewater-gates, our clever little plans to deceive and fool even our loved ones.

Now let me ask you several questions all in a row. As we look at these four definitions, I ask you: Are you a sinner? Obviously the answer is Yes. You are; I am; we all are. Most of us fall and fail with all four definitions. We're rebels; we miss the mark; we have an inner core of evil, and we have a deceptive streak.

And now God calls us to be perfect, to overcome sin. He wants us to experience obedience. And the Bible describes those in the last days, as we read in the book of Revelation, who are perfect. So let me ask: is it possible in this life for you and me to gain the victory over any of these kinds of sin? According to any of these definitions, can the people of God be perfect?

I'd like to take us back to the wedding chapel as we watch that bride come down the aisle toward her lover, her betrothed. She's beautiful, she's lovely, she's the picture of perfection. She's a bride adorned in all loveliness for the husband she loves.

However, two of these four definitions give us something to think about. We talked about sin as falling short, of having human limitations, of not being able to do all that a man or woman should be able to do. Would my bride, Jeannie Jones, ever fall short? Would she come to the end of the honeymoon and honestly be able to say, "I did *every* loving deed possible during this two-week trip. I accomplished every single thing a bride should do"? Or would she fall short once in a while simply because she's human? And would a loving bridegroom hold that against her?

Let's move to the definition that describes our inner "crookedness," our distorted moral beings. Jeannie Jones and yours truly, Lonnie Melashenko, and every other human on this planet possesses a sinful nature. *Inside* of us . . . we're sinners. No matter how we strive to obey, no matter how much we honestly do love the Lord Jesus Christ, we have humanness inside us; we have a sinful human nature. We may hate sin and love God—but until Jesus comes again and gives us glorified bodies and minds, we'll have that aspect of humanness, of sinfulness, to contend with. Any groom who stands in front of the church knows that a human bride is coming to meet him. He and she are both sinful human beings. From that narrow definition, they are not perfect . . . and will not be perfect in this life.

But the other two definitions of sin and sinfulness are something else altogether.

Let me ask you: how would you feel if your bride, your groom, offered you their hand in marriage—and yet you knew that their heart was filled with *pesha*, with rebellion? That they were planning warfare against you, plotting to overthrow you and wreak havoc on the marriage? What if your bride harbored *that* kind of sin?

Would God be willing to take into His kingdom a man or woman still filled with rebellious intentions? Would a person like that be safe to save?

In the fourth definition of sin—"guile" or "deception"—we have the same misgivings. Who would want to marry a sneaky, slippery, conniving, lying person who couldn't be trusted? Could God save someone who still clung to that kind of sin, that kind of imperfection?

Let me open my heart to you. When I got married, I married a woman who was perfect *in the ways that were important*. Jeannie brought loyalty to our marriage. She brought honesty and a forthright attitude. I knew I could trust her; I knew I had her loyalty and love. I knew it was safe to marry her.

She and I often fall short. We don't do all that we could do or that we should do. And she and I both possess human hearts and an inner crookedness that's our birthright inherited from Adam. We look forward to being healed of that. But we don't want to be rebels any longer.

Roy Adams quotes the hymnwriter, Mrs. C. H. Morris: "My stubborn will at last has yielded. I would be thine and thine alone. And this the prayer my lips are bringing: 'Lord, let in me Thy will be done. Sweet will of God, still fold me closer, Till I am wholly lost in Thee.' "

Then he closes by observing: "Those who come to the place where these words truly reflect the sentiments of the heart are on the way to heaven. With them, all transgressions, all revolt against God, all willful defiance of His rule have ceased. With them, rebellion will not arise the second time. They are *safe to save*."

CHAPTER 19

The Bridegroom's Fuzzy Bifocals

It's a common point of interest and even humor in literature and television that people about to be married have a different viewpoint than anybody else. They see things differently; they hear them differently; they feel them differently. Their senses are radically altered.

Everybody else who's part of the picture might see this fault or that upcoming pitfall or some other dilemma bigger than the proverbial nose on your face. But the bride and the groom—their matching rose-colored glasses keep them from seeing any potential problem.

Every time Mary Richards had a boyfriend on the *Mary Tyler Moore* show, you can bet that Lou Grant and Murray and Georgette and even Ted Baxter could see the problems a mile off. This fellow wasn't good enough for Mary; they knew what his flaws were. But could Mary see them? Not a chance. That's the way it is with love.

The Bridegroom's Fuzzy Bifocals

As I've said, a bride strives for perfection on her wedding day. And certainly, when her betrothed husband-to-be looks down the aisle and sees her coming toward him, that's what he sees. He has eyes that see only perfect loveliness.

Let's explore together the attitudes and the hearts of those two people. What are their motivations? What are they seeking? How do they react to each other?

We find one of the Bible's most eloquent pictures in the book of Genesis, where Jacob is looking for a wife. And he's fallen in love with a certain someone special. In Genesis 29:18, he makes this offer to his employer, Laban: "I'll work for you seven years in return for your younger daughter Rachel."

Seven years! Now here was one lovestruck fellow. He had eyes only for this young woman, who was, as the Bible puts it, "lovely in form, and beautiful." "Wellfavored," it says in the King James Version (verse 17).

Now, what did Jacob see when he looked at Rachel? He saw perfection! Perfect loveliness, perfect beauty, perfect everything. If Rachel had faults, he certainly didn't notice what they were. Jacob's bifocals seemed only to be in focus when he was looking at the loveliness of Laban's younger daughter.

In fact, we see just how faulty Jacob's eyesight really is when he accidentally marries the wrong daughter and even spends a honeymoon night with Leah without noticing anything wrong. Apparently it was dark in the bridal suite or honeymoon tent, and it's not until the next morning when he puts on his glasses and sees that something is terribly wrong. But he agrees to spend another seven years of work in order to get the perfect bride he really wants. Now that's a man who's seriously in love.

I believe that the God who's looking for perfection in His bride, the church of Christ, has those kinds of eyes. He's in love! He has the heart and the eyes of a Jacob! He's not looking for the blemishes and areas of falling short. His loving eyes are looking for a bride who is loyal and honest and willing to give herself unreservedly to this new relationship.

I like how the prophet Jeremiah describes the attitude of God—the Bridegroom God, if you will. "I have loved you with an everlasting love; I have drawn you with loving-kindness" (31:3).

How else does the Bible describe the attitude of God? Second Peter 3:9 has to be mentioned: "The Lord . . . is patient with you, not wanting anyone to perish, but everyone to come to repentance."

Do you see here a God who indeed looks for perfection in His saints—and yet exhibits incredible patience and a loving heart that sees past warts and flaws and looks for a loyal heart?

Make no mistake, friend; the Bible speaks very earnestly about perfection. The last three chapters contain clear Bible passages about God's people who obey in *all* areas, who have hearts that are totally pure. They are blameless, the Bible says. Without fault. Spiritually they are virgins, we read in Revelation 14.

And yet, as we've explored together, our focus needs to be on a personal *relationship* more than on personal achievement. Recognizing that God is looking more for loyalty than for a list of victories, we're invited to participate with Him in allowing His perfection to become ours. You remember the C. S. Lewis line where our Saviour promises: "Make no mistake: this is something *I Will Do* in you. *I Will* take you to that point."

Let me ask you a very pointed question which needs to penetrate every heart. *We* are the bride; every one of us. What is *our* attitude toward this topic of perfection? How do we feel about the Bride*groom*? How do we want to make ourselves ready for Him?

How did Rachel, in our Bible story, get ready for her wedding day?

The Bridegroom's Fuzzy Bifocals

Let's be very frank. A bride works hard, doesn't she? She spends long hours, days, even weeks and months to get ready for this wonderful, precious moment.

A wedding day involves more than just those ninety minutes in a dressing room getting the hair and the gown just right. No, a bride who's truly in love devotes everything she has to making sure she's ready. Months before the wedding she may go on a diet; she may get on an exercise program and jog four miles a day or hike up her StairMaster every night to make sure she's at her loveliest.

She may spend a whole year planning and preparing so that every aspect of the big day will be perfect. The dresses, the flowers, the decorations, everything. She spares no expense, no effort.

And there's something else too. Other men may come by with favors and gifts and seductive promises. She turns them down. She resists their temptations. She holds herself in purity, reserving herself and her gift of virginity for the man she loves. She obeys that commandment of love . . . so that she *can* fully love when her time comes.

All of this sounds like a lot of *work*, doesn't it? A lot of old-fashioned obeying, a striving for perfection. Is this perfectionism? Has she fallen into a checklist mentality, striving breathlessly to please and satisfy a vengeful, mean-spirited drill sergeant of a groom?

There's a tough-sounding verse in Philippians 2:12 where Paul tells the believers: "Therefore, my dear friends, as you have always obeyed—not only in my presence, but now much more in my absence—continue to *work out* your salvation with fear and trembling."

Wow! Those are challenging words! Here Paul, who spent his life telling people salvation was a free gift of God, now tells believers to work out that salvation. But I think he's simply recognizing the fact that involvement in a love relationship, preparing for a wedding, does indeed involve some work. It involves some getting ready.

What about the "fear and trembling" part? Was Paul afraid of his Lord and Saviour? Of course not! Paul spoke with confidence about God and about his own assurance of salvation. But isn't preparing for something as important as a wedding pretty serious business? Maybe you would shake a little bit as you applied the finishing touches to that wedding dress. "I hope he likes it," you say . . . and there *is* a bit of tremble to your voice as you anticipate the wonder of the upcoming moment.

Is that a fair interpretation? As I read all that God's Word has to say on the topic of perfection, I see that God's great saints of Bible times *wanted* to be perfect. They strove for perfection; they determined in their hearts to obey. But it didn't cause them anxiety and fear; rather, it brought them the same kind of intense joy that a bride experiences who is getting ready for her long march down that white-ribboned aisle.

Several times over the air I've read a very special passage from a *Voice of Prophecy* favorite: *Mere Christianity*, by C. S. Lewis. Perhaps you recall how he describes the happiness of those who obey, not in order to get saved, but in gratitude because they *are* saved. He paints a picture of their obeying "in a new, less-worried way." What a beautiful metaphor for God's people here in these last days!

One of the great, visionary pioneers in my own Adventist denomination was a special woman. Her name was Ellen White, and she's one of the most prolific writers in the Christian church. We've quoted her often on the *Voice of Prophecy*, and many of you have asked for copies of some of her books.

She wrote quite a bit about the topic of Christian perfection and about God's saints in the last days being pure and spotless. And some people have, maybe in a misguided way, looked at *her* life and her attitudes and her spiritual condition. Did she attain perfection? Did she overcome everything?

Let me share a couple of paragraphs that she wrote during her final illness back in the year 1915. "I do not say that I am perfect," she writes, "but I am *trying* to be perfect. I do not expect others to be perfect; and if I could not associate with my brothers and sisters who are not perfect, I do not know what I should do.

"I try to treat the matter the best that I can, and am thankful that I have a spirit of uplifting and not a spirit of crushing down. . . . No one is perfect. If one were perfect, he would be prepared for heaven. As long as we are not perfect, we have a work to do to get ready to be perfect. We have a mighty Saviour."

Isn't that just like a young bride? Not perfect . . . but she *wanted* to be perfect for the sake of her beloved. She tried hard to be perfect because she sensed how richly she was loved. And above all, her eyes were on her mighty Saviour.

CHAPTER 20

God's Stadium Card Trick

David Smith here.] Let me share an experience that occurred shortly before my wedding. May 11, 1980, was the big day—but a few weeks earlier my fiancée and I had to go down to the bank to fill out some papers for our joint banking accounts.

Well, for years Lisa had signed her name Lisa Jean *Ford*. But now, anticipating the new name she was soon going to have, the bank teller asked her to sign all the forms using her new name.

And what a special moment it was when she wrote down for the very first time: "Lisa Jean *Smith*." And then she kind of looked up at me and smiled. That was something I've never forgotten, even these sixteen-plus years later. How my bride was willing to accept that new name, that new identity. That she was willing to be known as my wife, my partner, my helpmeet. She accepted that new name.

As we've explored the concept of being Christ's bride and accepting the perfection He means for us to have, I can't help but feel that this special moment is part of that process. As Christians, we accept a new name, a new identity. We become publicly known for this new commitment. *We are Christ's*! And we gladly take our new name, which lets the whole world know. We want to spray-paint it all over town. [Lonnie, back to you!]

You know, my Adventist denomination and, really, every Christian body, has had to wrestle with a blunt two-word question: Why obey? If obedience and perfection don't *earn* you salvation, and if they aren't the necessary ingredients in keeping your salvation—then why do it? Why struggle? Why fight the good fight? Who cares about perfection?

But do you know something? That debate totally misses the point. For someone who is intensely in love, and who anticipates the joy of being God's spiritual bride, obedience follows naturally—for two important and wonderful reasons.

First, obedience does help nurture and strengthen the relationship. We explore that truth often on the *Voice of Prophecy*. God's commandments are a blueprint for a thriving love relationship with Him.

But the second reason is even more compelling; at least I think so. When we accept that new name, and enter into that new relationship, then we seek perfection because it *honors* that name. It honors God.

Let me tell you again about a Bible verse I think we all should memorize. It's not especially profound except for the fact that it always fixes our mixed-up human ideas about why we should obey. It's found in Matthew 5:16: "Let your light so shine before men, that they may see your good works, and glorify your Father which is in heaven" (KJV).

"Obey My Father's commandments," Jesus tells us. Why? Because it makes *God* look good! Your obedience honors Him; it uplifts Him and gives legitimacy to His kingdom. It makes a relationship with Him attractive to others.

What a beautiful motivation this provides! In fact, it's the only motivation that really *can* produce genuine obedience and perfection. Any other kind of perfection-seeking quickly turns into an ugly, inward-gazing, and soon vicious exercise in spiritual pride.

We've mentioned the Bible references to people who were perfect, as Scripture described them. Noah was a perfect man. So was Job. But there's another who was described as perfect: "You were perfect, blameless, in your ways from the day you were created" (28:15).

That's how the book of Ezekiel describes this person. Do you know who it's talking about? That's right; it's talking about the devil. Lucifer—who was created perfect by God. The last half of the verse adds: "You were perfect . . . till wickedness was found in you."

Here was a being who was perfect! But did that created angel allow his perfection to bring glory to God? Or did he begin to be proud of his perfection—and then it wasn't perfection any longer? It's something to think about, isn't it?

Let's never fall into the trap of gazing at our perfection. The Bible does tell us, "Be perfect, as your heavenly Father is perfect," but let's not compare ourselves to God. Any perfection God gives us is for the purpose of *honoring* God, not comparing ourselves with Him. I love how the writer A. W. Tozer says in his book, *The Knowledge of the Holy*: "Holy is the way God is. To be holy He does not conform to a standard. He *is* that standard."

Lucifer tried to be as perfect as God; he wanted to be *as* God. Let's never fall into that foolish and fatal trap. Any goodness we have is given to us by God, for the purpose of bringing honor to His own name.

Now, as our journey together draws to its close, will you allow your thoughts to travel with me to the book in the back of your Bible? We have a special love for the book of Revelation here at the *Voice of Prophecy*. And you can understand that from our name: Voice of *Prophecy*. We're interested in the prophecies of the last days; we like to turn to these last twenty-two chapters and encourage our listeners with the good news that Jesus is coming soon. Right now I have to share my personal conviction that He's coming *very* soon.

And here in these mysterious but marvelous last pages, we find a picture of God's people. These people *together* make up the bride of Christ. And they have a kind of perfection. Especially in chapter 14 we can read about this special group. They sing a new song because they've been redeemed by the blood of the Lamb. The cross of Calvary means everything to them; they think of it and ponder its grandeur and meaning all the time. And because of the cross, they love that Lamb of God; verse 4 says they follow the Lamb everywhere He goes. They're faultless before the throne of God; blameless; perfect. There's no guile, no deception, no lies or falsehoods in their mouths. These are men and women, thinking mature Christians who have an intense, burning passion, a love for their God.

And their goodness honors God. Their obedience brings glory, not to themselves, but to the God they love. And that's exactly how they want it to be. They've been through the persecution and the plagues of Revelation; they've experienced unbelievable challenges and even torment . . . and their loyalty has never wavered. What a sight for the onlooking world and the watching universe!

It's often been suggested that these last-day saints are a reflection, even a *perfect* reflection, of the character of Jesus Himself. And that's a beautiful thought—but it could undo everything we've talked about in this book. It could bring us right back to doubts and fears and a selfish kind of competitive inward-gazing that destroys the wedding atmosphere we've looked forward to.

[David again.] May I share with you my stadium card illustration? Sometimes at a college football game, especially a big televised bowl game, everyone in attendance is given a series of large colored cards. It's all been computer-arranged, so that you're sitting in the right place with the right cards. And at the precise moment when a signal is given, you hold up your cards. Maybe a huge picture of the school mascot appears. Or the school slogan. Or a picture of a new Chevy truck. But as every person holds up his or her cards, *together* with everyone in the stadium, a perfect picture appears that you can see all the way up in the Goodyear blimp.

I believe that all God's people *together*—living in these last days—can reflect the perfection that God longs to see in His people. You, in your love and loyalty for Jesus, hold up your card. Lonnie and I hold up ours. Still others all around the globe are joyfully living for their Saviour, obeying Him, demonstrating their fierce loyalty to Him through whatever trials may come.

Can you, reading these words wherever you are, all by yourself be *as perfect* as Jesus? Let's not even think that way. If you were as perfect as Jesus, you wouldn't need Jesus. But what a wonderful thought that all of us together, obeying and accepting God's gift of perfection—*together* we can be that picture of perfection to the watching universe!

Of course, just like in that college football stadium, you need every participant there. You can't come late; you can't leave early. You can't take a break to go out and buy popcorn or a hotdog. You're needed in your place at the right time, ready to hold up that card.

Today God's calling you to His demonstration. He's calling you to be a part of the bride of Christ, to join with countless others in *together* reflecting the perfect character of Jesus. He needs you; we all need you. The wedding pictures won't be complete without you.

The bridal invitations have all been mailed out. What's your response going to be?